Stukeley Illustrated

First published 2003.
This second edition is published by

Green Magic
5 Stathe Cottages
Stathe

www.greenmagicpublishing.com
info@greenmagicpublishing.com

Typeset by K.DESIGN, Winscombe, Somerset

Cover from
William Stukeley's Stonehenge: A Temple Restor'd to the British Druids,
'A peep into the sanctum sanctorum'. The back cover shows a
detail from 'The Cove of the Northern Temple' in
Abury, A Temple of the British Druids.

Stukeley Illustrated

William Stukeley's Rediscovery of Britain's Ancient Sites

Compiled by

Neil Mortimer

Green Magic

A 1721 portrait of Stukeley, reproduced in the Surtees Society's *Family Memoirs of Rev. William Stukeley vol. 1*, 1882.

Contents

William Stukeley, 1687–1765   1

Stonehenge   9

Avebury   41

Itinerarium Curiosum   79

Postscript   124

William Stukeley Bibliography   130

Further Reading   131

Index of Sites and Places in the Engravings   134

Acknowledgements

William Stukeley has inadvertently introduced me to some people it's been a pleasure to know. The first time I saw a drawing of Stukeley's, it was being slide projected by Rob Stephenson of the London Earth Mysteries Circle during a talk he was giving at the City University, London. Pete Glastonbury, Brian Edwards and Julian Cope have all stuck up for Stukeley in Wiltshire. John Chandler brought James Davis to my attention in *The Day Returns* (Ex Libris Press, 1998). Bob Trubshaw came up trumps with a last minute query about Roman Leicestershire. John Michell opened up an agreeable world in *Megalithomania*, and David Boyd Haycock's biography of Stukeley opened up a new one much later. I didn't know Stuart Piggott, but after reading his biography of Stukeley I was hooked. Jezza Harte offered very useful advice along the way as usual. Aubrey Burl has done more than anyone else to inspire the 'yearning of ruins' in a generation or more of stone crawlers. Thanks Aubrey. Without Schrafftafari, it's unlikely that any of this would have happened, and if it had it would have made much less sense.

Introduction

William Stukeley's position as one of the earliest archaeological fieldworkers was confirmed by archaeologists' rediscovery of the Beckhampton Avenue at Avebury in the summer of 1999. The excavation of the ancient megalithic avenue, which many observers once wrote off as a product of Stukeley's overheated imagination, was a reminder that Stukeley was an honest and reliable recorder of the remarkable prehistoric monuments he visited during the 18th century.

But Stukeley is known for more than his archaeological fieldwork, and he is honoured and sometimes damned for the part he played in the druidical revival of the 18th century. This is in no small part due to the engravings, prepared from Stukeley's sketches, drawings and watercolours, that accompany the text of his best known books. It is this visual aspect of Stukeley's work that *Stukeley Illustrated* celebrates; from the evocative romanticism of some of his illustrations of prehistoric sites to the excellent technical draughtsmanship of others.

As well as their archaeological and historical value, Stukeley's two most celebrated published works, *Stonehenge, A Temple Restor'd to the British Druids* (1740) and *Abury, A Temple of the British Druids, With Some Others Described* (1743) are collectible and highly sought after books in their own right. They have been reprinted only twice; once in 1838 editions which are now almost as scarce as the original 18th century editions, and again in a more recent joint edition published in the United States in 1982, which is almost impossible to find. Other Stukeley volumes, most notably the wonderful *Itinerarium Curiosum*, first published in 1724 and later reprinted in a greatly expanded edition of 1776, are also covered in *Stukeley Illustrated*. Images drawn from a handful of miscellaneous sources are noted in the picture captions as appropriate. It is worth noting that this book does not attempt to draw together any of the wealth of unpublished Stukeley sketches and illustrations that survive, and instead concentrates on the published engravings that feature in his three main original publications.

One of the reasons for the scarcity of Stukeley's books is their enormous visual appeal. Sadly, this has resulted in many original copies being broken up and the engravings removed and sold as individual prints. *Stukeley Illustrated* cannot rival the charms of the original volumes, complete with folding plates and *Abury*'s quarter folded frontispiece, but it provides a more portable substitute for those magnificent and now very expensive books.

A surprising amount is known about Stukeley's life and work. This is in no small part due to the great archaeologist Stuart Piggott, whose 1950 biography *William Stukeley: An Eighteenth-Century Antiquary*, did much to return Stukeley to the antiquarian map and was the foundation upon which much of the modern interest in Stukeley was formed. Thames & Hudson published a second edition of Piggott's biography of Stukeley in 1985, and this edition of the book is still widely available. *Stukeley Illustrated* was originally conceived as an illustrated biography, but during the early stages of preparation a new scholarly biography of Stukeley was published, David Boyd Haycock's *William Stukeley: Science, Religion and Archaeology in Eighteenth-Century England* (Boydell, 2002). The publication of Haycock's account of Stukeley's life has meant that there is rather more 'illustrated' and rather less 'biography' in *Stukeley Illustrated*. While the most noteworthy events of Stukeley's life are covered in *Stukeley Illustrated*, readers wanting to delve more deeply into all things Stukeley are directed to both Piggott's and Haycock's books, which offer two quite different interpretations of his work. Details of other useful publications are included in the Further Reading section at the end of this book.

Finally, a note about the quality of reproductions in *Stukeley Illustrated*. I have tried to source the best quality originals wherever possible, but in some instances less than perfect quality images were the best that could be obtained. Therefore slightly poorer quality engravings featuring particularly interesting subject matter have been included in a handful of instances.

Neil Mortimer
Devizes - July, 2003

1

William Stukeley, 1687–1765

As important as he is to the modern history of prehistoric sites, the English anti-quarian William Stukeley was not the first to investigate the ancient monuments that are still scattered throughout the British Isles today. Thousands of years before the antiquarians, in prehistory, people were interested in the monuments that their ancestors had created hundreds or even thousands of years earlier. Monuments raised in the Neolithic period (*c.* 4,200 to 2,200 BC) were appropriated, sometimes rearranged or added to, and certainly regarded as special and probably magical to the later Bronze Age (*c.* 2,200 to 800 BC) peoples to whom the sites were already ancient. As new monuments were erected in stone, earth and timber, so the process continued, through the Iron Age (*c.* 800 BC to 43 AD) and into Roman times (*c.* 43 AD to 410 AD) by which time some ancient sites already had a real and mythic history of several thousand years. And the attention afforded to these mysterious places carried on beyond the Romans into the Anglo-Saxon period (*c.* 450 AD to 1066 AD), when monuments, some approaching 4,000 years old, were renamed in honour of Norse Gods. By the 12th century, Stonehenge on Salisbury Plain, Wiltshire, entered Britain's cultural patchwork as a potent symbol of the collective past when Henry of Huntingdon made the first written reference to the site in 1130.

The 16th century saw the rise of a new method of unravelling the distant past. Antiquarianism took many forms, but much of the research centred on attempts to make sense of the apparent chaos of ancient history using the works of the classical authors, such as Caesar and Tacitus, who both wrote about the druids in Iron Age Britain. The increasing contact with 'primitive' societies around the globe, caused by the expansion of trading and trade routes, also provided a rich vein of information to be tapped.

In 1586 William Camden published *Britannia*, the first attempt to account for the most significant ancient remains that still existed in Britain. Antiquaries sprang up across Europe, such as Ole Worm in Denmark, who made records of ancient sites in his own country, and Olof Rudbeck in Sweden, who undertook an early form of archaeological excavation. In Britain, historical research into Roman remains and Saxon history was already established, but as the 17th century progressed antiquarians increasingly turned their attentions to prehistory. Aylett Sammes, John Anstis, Thomas Gale (later followed by his two sons, Roger and Samuel), Edward Lhuyd, Robert Plot and John Toland all made important contributions to the study of pre-Roman Britain, but among them one person, John Aubrey (1626–97), was the most pioneering. Along with Stukeley, Aubrey's research did the most to widen interest in prehistoric monuments during the 17th and 18th centuries. In 1649 Aubrey became the first person to document the huge prehistoric site of Avebury, lying on the chalk uplands of the Marlborough Downs in Wiltshire. His seemingly unquenchable thirst for natural and man-made curiosities led him to make drafts of prehistoric field monuments that were collated in his hugely influential manuscript *Monumenta Britannica*, which would not be published in its entirety until the end of the 20th century. In 1695 Edmund Gibson published a vastly expanded English edition of Camden's *Britannia*, which inspired a new wave of antiquarian researchers, of which William Stukeley would be at the forefront.

William Stukeley was born in Holbeach, Lincolnshire, on Monday, November 7, 1687. More than 300 years later he would be revered as the founder of landscape archaeology and recognised as one of the main inspirations behind the druidical revival of the 19th century.

Stukeley was the eldest son in a family of four boys and one girl; his father was employed in the family law firm. When he was five years old Stukeley started attending the Free School at Holbeach, where he learnt the rudiments of drawing which would be so important to him later in life, and by age 13 he was excelling academically. In the same year, 1700, Stukeley joined the family law firm, but he soon realized that this was not an occupation he wanted to pursue. Stukeley persuaded his father to allow him to go to university in order to study medicine and in 1703 he went to Bene't College in Cambridge, later renamed Corpus Christi College.

In 1706, when Stukeley was 19, his father died. This was soon followed by the death of one of his brothers and his uncle – the other partner in the family firm. Because he was the eldest son, Stukeley needed to return to the family home in Lincolnshire to help his mother and brothers sort out the family's affairs. He returned to his studies at Cambridge, but the following year in 1707, another brother and his mother passed away, and once again Stukeley needed to return to the family home, this time as the guardian of his remaining younger brothers and sister. During this stay in Holbeach, Stukeley caused a stir when he dissected the corpse of a local man who had killed himself and been buried in a roadside grave. It would not be the last time that Stukeley took an opportunity to carry out a post-mortem in unusual circumstances.

While studying medicine, the first signs of Stukeley's interest in ancient monuments began to awaken, and he made drawings of notable examples of architecture during his time in Cambridge. In 1709, aged 22, his studies took him to London to study at St Thomas's Hospital, under the tutorship of the distinguished physician Dr. Richard Mead, who shared with Stukeley a keen interest in antiquities. Stukeley tired of the city after less than a year and returned to Lincolnshire to take up a country practice in Boston. During the next decade, Stukeley's enthusiasm for the ancient past would develop enormously.

Stukeley joined the recently inaugurated Gentleman's Society of Spalding, whose members would meet or remain in contact by letter with the intention of exploring 'natural and artificial curiosities'. While not a specifically antiquarian association, the Society counted amongst its members some of the leading antiquarians of the day, including Roger and Samuel Gale, Sir John Clerk and the Scottish antiquary Alexander Gordon. Stukeley would have been particularly pleased that his hero, Sir Isaac Newton (1642–1727), was also a member. Stukeley's multifarious interests now included antiquities, astronomy, architecture, natural history, botany, geography, music, history and theology, and there is no doubt that he would have enjoyed this environment of gentlemanly scholarship a great deal.

Between the years 1710 and 1725 Stukeley undertook a series of tours of Britain, which saw him visiting ancient and notable sites throughout the land. It was during these tours, domestic equivalents of the Grand Tour of Europe, that Stukeley carried out the preliminary fieldwork that would fuel his love of prehistoric antiquities. The journeys initially took in churches, cathedrals, follies and natural landmarks, but as the years progressed, visits to prehistoric stone circles, barrows and earthworks came to dominate the tours. Illustrated accounts of the earlier tours were published in the first edition of Stukeley's *Itinerarium Curiosum* (1724). The book left out Stukeley's then recent fieldwork at Stonehenge and Avebury. Accounts of this groundbreaking research would have to wait a further 15 years to be published.

In 1717, after a period of relative obscurity in the country, Stukeley, now 30 years old, returned to London where he remade connections with former acquaintances and threw himself into metropolitan antiquarian life. In 1718 he was made a Fellow of the Royal Society, of which Sir Isaac Newton was president. The newly formed Society of Antiquaries, which had met on an informal basis for ten years or so, became a formal institution soon after and Stukeley was elected the society's first secretary.

During 1717 or 1718, Stukeley read a manuscript that was to shape the rest of his life. A colleague passed him a copy of John Aubrey's *Monumenta Britannica*, the legendary unpublished manuscript of proto-archaeological observations of ancient sites made more than half a century earlier. Stukeley read and transcribed lengthy sections of the manuscript but, curiously, did not acknowledge Aubrey's enormously important achievements in his own published works. In 1719 Stukeley visited Stonehenge and Avebury for the first time, the start of half a decade of fieldwork carried out during the summer months which would ultimately lead to the publishing of the two books that Stukeley is rightly most renowned for, *Stonehenge, A Temple Restor'd to the British Druids* (1740) and *Abury, A Temple of the British Druids, With Some Others Described* (1743).

In 1722 Stukeley formed the 'Society of Roman Knights', a circle of scholarly gentlemen dedicated to the study of Roman Britain, and as an alternative to the medieval gothic concerns which prevailed amongst members of the recently founded Society of Antiquaries. The Roman Knights took the names of historical or literary figures from which they drew inspiration; Stukeley's name was Chyndonax, from a Greek inscription recorded on a glass urn that had been discovered in 1598. Fanciful speculation that the name was that of a druid priest interested Stukeley, and *Stonehenge* included a self-portrait of him striking a classical-druidic pose as Chyndonax (see p.13).

While antiquarian matters were preoccupying Stukeley, he was still a practising doctor of medicine. One of his more unusual medical assignments took place in 1720 when a captive elephant which had recently died in London became available for dissection. Apparently the animal's death had been speeded by the 'great quantity of ale that the spectators continually gave it'. Stukeley did not pass over the opportunity to examine the dead elephant, and the results of the procedure were published in 1723.

The Grand Lodge of Freemasonry was formally established in 1717, and Stukeley became a freemason at the Salutation Tavern, Tavistock Street, London. Stukeley was particularly interested in ideas then current that the roots of Freemasonry might be found in antiquity, perhaps even in the early pagan religions. Some of these notions would influence Stukeley's beliefs about ancient sites and druids later in his life.

Soon after the *Itinerarium Curiosum* was published in 1724 Stukeley's serious fieldwork came to an end, and for the rest of his life he preferred to contemplate the ancient past from his desk rather than in the field. In 1726 he left London once again and returned to his native Lincolnshire to work as a country doctor. In 1727 he married Frances Williamson, and within a few years his life would take an unexpected turn. Whether it was a response to deeply held religious convictions or simply that his financial circumstances demanded it, in 1729, aged 42, Stukeley was ordained into the Church of England and became the vicar of All Saints, Stamford. Certainly theological matters had always interested Stukeley, but it is equally likely that the life and salary of a country doctor had proved to be unfulfilling to his restless, enquiring mind. Certainly the gentleman's lifestyle of a rector would have perfectly suited Stukeley's extracurricular interests in ancient sites.

Along with this change of occupation and circumstance came a change in preoccupation. Stukeley began to shape his earlier fieldwork into a complex religious theory that the Britons of antiquity, and more specifically the druids, were practitioners of a proto-Christian religion who had fallen into paganism after contact with continental heathens. By promoting this misguided but then current theory, Stukeley famously hoped to 'combat the deists from an unexpected quarter'. Stukeley was concerned by the religious modernisation that was taking place during this period, and in particular the potentially dangerous deist philosophy of Natural Religion, that God created the universe but did not interfere with humanity and favoured no religion over another.

At Stamford, away from his religious duties, Stukeley busied himself writing and gardening, another of his lifelong passions. His most significant task of the late 1720s and early 1730s was preparing the text and illustrations for *Stonehenge* and *Abury*. Stukeley originally wrote the manuscripts in the early 1720s while his fieldwork was still underway, and in this later period edited them, inserting passages that reflected his current interests throughout. While the engravings were in the main prepared based on sketches and plans made in the field, the texts of the books were very different to the books Stukeley had envisaged 15 or so years before.

In 1737 Stukeley's first wife passed away, leaving him three daughters to look after. In 1739, aged 50, he married Elizabeth Gale, the sister of his fellow antiquarians Roger and Samuel Gale, receiving a £10,000 wedding dowry. This financial improvement allowed Stukeley to keep two houses, one at Stamford and another in London where he spent winters with his second wife and daughters. Sadly, the marriage was not a happy one because, as one later commentator had it, Stukeley had married 'Discord'.

In 1747, a few years after *Abury* was published, Stukeley was offered a position at the church of St George's, Queen's Square, Bloomsbury in London. Stukeley accepted, but shortly before he left for the city he received a letter of great interest from Charles Julius Bertram, an Englishman residing in Denmark. Bertram informed Stukeley that he had come into the possession of a manuscript fragment of an account of Roman Britain written by a 14th century monk called

Richard of Cirencester. This now infamous document turned out to be one of the most notorious literary forgeries ever carried out. Despite being cautious of the document, Stukeley – along with just about every other scholar of the era – was ultimately taken in by Bertram. In 1756, *An Account of Richard of Cirencester, Monk of Westminster, and of his Works* was published. The provenance of the manuscript would be discussed and debated for years, but it was not until almost 100 years later that it was definitively proved to be a literary fake. It will never be known why Bertram faked the manuscript; he earned little or no money from it and seemed to have been an enthusiastic and genuine fieldworker. Perhaps he wanted to make his mark on history and thought that if Stukeley could be interested in the manuscript it would be easier to publicise the 'discovery'.

During his own lifetime, Stukeley was not always held in the highest regard. Despite his pioneering work at Stonehenge and Avebury, by the middle of the 18th century his interest in religious matters began to make him look a little old-fashioned in learned circles. The view of antiquarians as dotty old men with insatiable appetites for trivia was already well established at the time. An obscure parochial example of a contemporary response to Stukeley can be found in the satirical *Origines Divisianae. Or the Antiquities of the Devizes: In Some Familiar Letters to a Friend. Wrote in the Years 1750, and 1751*, published anonymously in 1754 by an author later identified as Dr. James Davis of Devizes. 'I acknowledge an *Owl's* egg is an unusual magnitude for a medicinal dose: but it was thought here not too large, because all Students who are form'd by nature for antiquities are furnish'd with *large swallows*. I would have them like the family of the St__k__y's. You must be inform'd that there were two Williams, one was a physician at Grantham, the other a Divine at Stamford and London. They both descended from the ancient house of Stevekele, both their Christian and Sirnames were the same: and tho' they were both as like as Virgil's twins... Yet they were very different men. The Physician believ'd nothing but the most *incredible* things of the Celtic Gods; the other as appears by a late sermon preach'd before the College of Physicians, avowedly believes in the Devil and all his works.'

Despite the detractors, Stukeley's reputation remained solid among his antiquarian contemporaries, and both *Stonehenge* and *Abury* were well received. (For a recent examination of Stukeley's contemporary reputation, see David Boyd Haycock's article on this subject listed in the Further Reading section at the end of the book.)

Stukeley still published widely on ancient and other matters. A medical volume *Of the Gout* appeared in 1735, along with *The Philosophy of Earthquakes, Natural and Religious* in 1750. He prepared a biography of his old colleague Sir

Isaac Newton, which was not published until 1936. Coins continued to interest Stukeley, and in 1759 *The Medallic History of Marcus Aurelius Valerius Carausius* was published. A collection of Stukeley's sermons was included in 1763 as *Paleographia Sacra, or Discourses on Sacred Subjects.*

On the last day of February in 1765, at the age of 78, Stukeley went from his cottage in Kentish Town to the Rectory at Queen's Square to attend to some matter of business. While taking a rest on a couch, he suffered a stroke and fell into a coma which lasted for three days. Stukeley died finally on Sunday, March 3rd. He was buried in the churchyard at East Ham, Essex, and at his own request the grave was unmarked.

Some years after Stukeley's death, the antiquary William Warburton wrote a fitting tribute to Stukeley in a letter to a colleague: 'I have a tenderness in my temper which will make me miss poor Stukeley; for, not to say that he was one of my oldest acquaintance, there was in him such a mixture of simplicity, drollery, absurdity, ingenuity, superstition and antiquarianism, that he afforded me that kind of well-seasoned repast, which the French call an *Ambigu*, I suppose from a compound of things never meant to meet together. I have often heard him laughed at by fools, who had neither his sense, his knowledge, or his honesty; though it must be confessed, that in him they were all strangely travestied.'

STONEHENGE

A

TEMPLE

RESTOR'D

TO THE

𝔅𝔯𝔦𝔱𝔦𝔰𝔥 𝔇ℜ𝔘𝔍𝔇𝔖.

By *WILLIAM STUKELEY*, M. D.

Rector of *All Saints* in STAMFORD.

——Deus est qui non mutatur in ævo.   MANILIUS.

LONDON:

Printed for W. INNYS and R. MANBY, at the West End
of St. *Paul's.*

MDCCXL.

2

Stonehenge

'A few years ago I spent some time every summer in viewing, measuring, and considering the works of the ancient Druids in our Island; I mean those remarkable circles of Stone which we find all over the kingdom, many of which I have seen, but of many more I have had accounts. Their greatness and number astonish'd me, nor need I be afraid to say, their beauty and design, as well as antiquity, drew my particular attention. I could not help carrying my enquiries about them as far as I was able. My studies this way have produc'd a vast quantity of drawings and writing, which consider'd as an intire work, may thus be intitled, Patriarchal Christianity: or, A Chronological History of the Origin and Progress of the true Religion, and of Idolatry.'

From the preface to *Stonehenge, A Temple Restor'd*
to the British Druids (1740).

William Stukeley's *Stonehenge* may be the most notorious book ever written about the most famous stone circle in the world, but it was not the first. That honour falls to Inigo Jones, Charles I's court architect, whose *Stone-Heng Restored* was published in 1655, three years after his death. Here, Jones wrongly credited the Romans with Stonehenge's construction. Another three books solely about Stonehenge were published ahead of Stukeley's. Walter Charlton, King Charles II's physician, followed Jones in 1660 with *Chorea Gigantum; or, The Most Famous Antiquity of Great-Britan, Vulgarly called Stone-heng, Standing on Salisbury Plain, Restored to the Danes*. In 1665 John Webb published *A Vindication of 'Stone-Heng Restored'*, defending his deceased relative Inigo Jones' Roman theories. At the tail-end of this flurry of flawed books about Stonehenge came the obscure Somerset wit Robert Gay, whose bizarre and mocking *A Fool's Bolt Soon Shott at Stonage* was written in the 1660s but not printed until 1725. These writers variously attributed Stonehenge to Danes, Romans and even giants, and all were mistaken.

John Aubrey, Stukeley's most worthy predecessor, made good plans of Stonehenge in 1666, but due to the flighty nature of his research, they were buried in his muddled manuscript, the 'Monumenta Britannica', and their significance was largely unrecognised outside of the intellectual elite until much later.

With interest in Britain's distant past growing during the 17th century, so too did theories about the origins of ancient monuments. By the end of the century the fashion of attributing Stonehenge to Romans or ancient Danish builders was declining, and it was the turn of the Iron Age druids to be misassociated with Stonehenge's construction. Since the 19th century, John Aubrey has been collared with starting the association between megalithic monuments and druids, but it is likely that this was a concept that was 'in the air' within learned circles in the early 17th century. When it became clear that neither the Romans nor the Danes would have created a monument like Stonehenge, and once people accepted that Stonehenge was unlikely to have been assembled magically by Merlin or brutishly by giants, there were few options to take but to turn to the pre-Roman druids described in the classical allusions to them. In fact it was not until the 1950s and the introduction of radiocarbon dating that the idea of a druidical Stonehenge could be finally laid to rest.

William Stukeley first visited Stonehenge on 18 May 1719, and druids did not seem to be on his mind until some years later. Over the next five years he visited the monument many times during the summer months, surveying, sketching, taking draughts, drawing up plans and exploring the wider landscape of Stonehenge. Assisted by numerous antiquarian colleagues, including his aristocratic friend Lord Pembroke, Stukeley was the first to recognise Stonehenge's Avenue and Cursus, and made many important and hitherto unnoticed observations about the site itself. Stukeley was clearly in his element during antiquarian explorations in Wiltshire, writing 'it is time to draw toward the sacred pile, and fancy ourselves walking upon this delightful plain… nought can be sweeter than the air that moves o're this hard and dry, chalky soil. Every step you take upon the smooth carpet, (literally) your nose is saluted with the most fragrant smell of *serpillum*, and *apium,* which with the short grass continually cropt by the flocks of sheep, composes the softest and most verdant turf, extremely easy to walk on, and which rises as with a spring, under ones feet' and 'Salisbury Plain (as commonly call'd) for extent and beauty, is, without controversy, one of the most delightful parts of *Britain*'.

Stukeley attempted to unravel the origin and meaning of the name Stonehenge with mixed results. He argued against those earlier writers who had credited the Romans or Danes with Stonehenge's construction. He pondered the significance of the great post-Roman earthwork, Wansdyke, which cut an east-west boundary between Stonehenge and that other giant temple of Avebury to the north. Perhaps most significantly, Stukeley made a great number of sketches and drawings, which would later be engraved and reproduced in his published book. The wider landscape around Stonehenge was recorded in astonishing detail, and his sketches would not only make *Stonehenge* visually dazzling, but would also provide a priceless record of Stonehenge and its environs in the 1720s for later researchers.

Stukeley differed from the earlier writers in several important respects. He recognised that first hand observation and surveys of sites and the landscapes in which they stand was absolutely crucial, and in doing so he effectively invented field archaeology. Where earlier writers tended to rely on classical sources for their theories, Stukeley, at least initially, preferred to record what he actually saw in the field. After this great period of fieldwork more or less came to an end in the mid-1720s, so too did the most brilliant part of his long career. Stukeley's best work revolutionised the understanding and knowledge of Britain's prehistory. Inevitably, his later – and more overtly religious – research, while still busy and fruitful, were less distinguished. Stukeley intended *Stonehenge* to be the seventh and final volume of a series of books chronicling the history of Patriarchal Christianity. The only other volume in this projected series that he succeeded in publishing was the sixth, concerning Avebury. It is unlikely that the publication of the other five volumes would have added a great deal of worthwhile material to what had already appeared in *Stonehenge* and *Abury*.

Stukeley began writing up his work on Stonehenge during the 1720s while he was still engaged in fieldwork, but his book would not go to the press for years to come. The further in time Stukeley was away from his fieldwork, the more theological matters began to occupy his thoughts. By the time *Stonehenge* was published, his accounts of the discoveries he had made in the field on Salisbury Plain had been mixed with discussions of druids, patriarchal religion and Stukeley's belief that the Anglican Church was the heir to God's original and universal religion. The original fieldwork remained, but was wrapped in religious diversions that to some extent obscured the genius of his earlier work. Readers may be interested to know that a complete transcript of Stukeley's original and largely irreligious *Stonehenge* manuscript was published in 2004. (See the 'Further Reading' section at the end of this book.)

While the visual brilliance of Stukeley's *Stonehenge* has never been questioned, historically the text has been unfairly dismissed as the ramblings of a pseudo-druidical crank. But despite the theological intrusions, *Stonehenge* is a remarkable book. After its publication it remained the most important and accurate description of the site for 150 years, well into the period when archaeology was taking shape as a modern discipline. *Stonehenge* records Stukeley's observations of the site: its architecture, form, orientation, the different types of stone used, the possible building methods used in its construction and the previously unknown avenue attached to the site. Not only that, *Stonehenge* records the wider landscape of prehistoric sites, including the unrecognised cursus to the north of the monument and the great number and variety of barrows surrounding Stonehenge, some of which no longer exist. That Stukeley's words 'trilithon' and 'cursus' have passed into standard archaeological terminology and are still used today is just one example of how groundbreaking his work at Stonehenge was. There is more than enough in *Stonehenge* to consider it an unequivocal masterpiece.

If all that was known of Stukeley was his *Stonehenge*, he would still be rightly celebrated today. As it was, his most monumental and astonishing book was yet to come.

The frontispiece to *Stonehenge*. In this engraving Stukeley strikes a classical-druidic pose as Chyndonax, the name he took at the Society of Roman Knights.

A British Druid. The source of this iconic image can be traced via Henry Rowlands' *Mona Antiqua Restaurata* (1723) to Aylett Sammes' *Britannia Antiqua Illustrata* (1676).

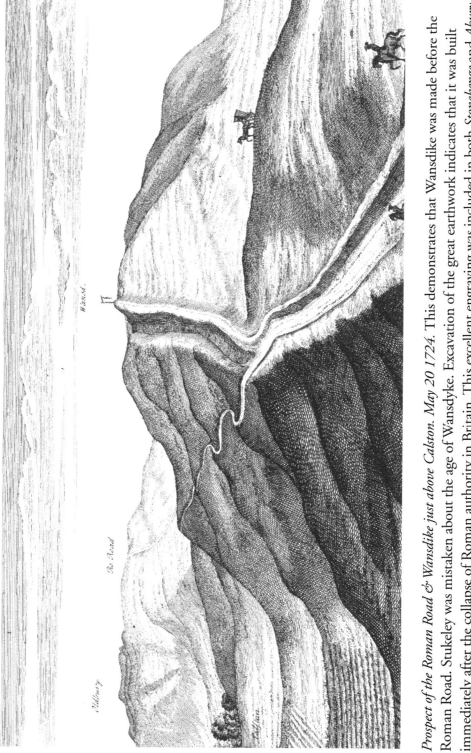

Prospect of the Roman Road & Wansdike just above Calston. May 20 1724. This demonstrates that Wansdike was made before the Roman Road. Stukeley was mistaken about the age of Wansdyke. Excavation of the great earthwork indicates that it was built immediately after the collapse of Roman authority in Britain. This excellent engraving was included in both *Stonehenge* and *Abury*.

15

Prospect of Stonehenge from the east by Vespasians camp. (detail) This is the view of Stonehenge that would have greeted travellers approaching the monument from Amesbury. Vespasian's Camp is an Iron Age hillfort which lies east of Amesbury alongside the A303.

A View a little beyond Woodyates where the Ikening Street crosses part of a Druids barrow. June 9 1724. Icknield Street, or Ackling Dyke, is an exceptionally well-preserved Roman road which runs from Old Sarum in Wiltshire across Cranborne Chase to Badbury Rings in Dorset. Stukeley observed 'British' monuments that had been cut through by Roman structures, and realised that they must have preceded the Roman era.

The Front view of Stonehenge. The first close-up view of Stonehenge in Stukeley's book, looking southwest along the monument's primary axis. Stukeley often included himself and his colleagues in his drawings – note the antiquarians taking records.

A peep into the Sanctum Sanctorum. 6 June 1724. This superb portrayal of an imaginary druidic ceremony captures the special atmosphere inside Stonehenge, and shows that even while on flights of fancy Stukeley remained an excellent draughtsman.

Top: *North Prospect from Stonehenge.*   Bottom: *Southwest Prospect from Stonehenge.*

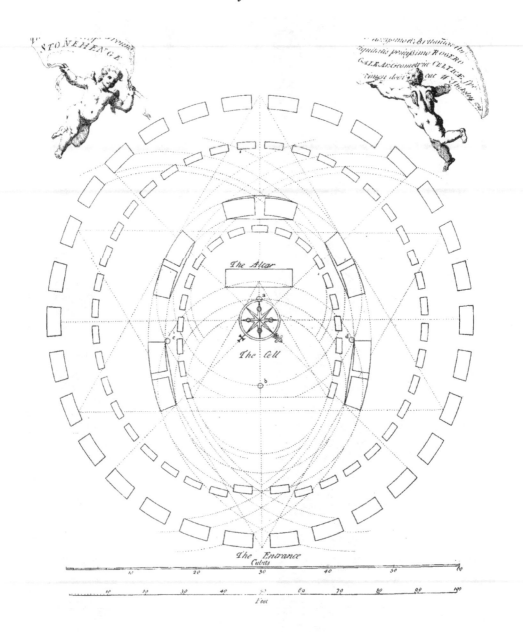

The Geometrical Groundplot of Stonehenge. This engraving was the first accurate plan published of the site as it would have stood before ruination.

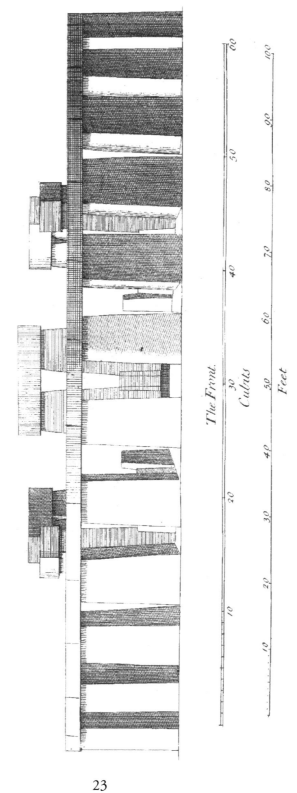

The Orthography of Stonehenge. Stukeley produced four technically precise drawings of the outer appearance of Stonehenge in this style.

23

A direct view of the remains of the adytum of Stonehenge. The adytum, or innermost part of the temple, is framed by the sarsen trilithon and bluestone horseshoe arrangements of stones.

Inward view of Stonehenge from the high altar. August 1722. Looking northeast along Stonehenge's axis towards the outer bluestone and lintelled sarsen circles. The trilithon on the right of the engraving is the easterly outer spur of the sarsen horseshoe.

An inward view of Stonehenge. August 1722 from the north. *(detail)*

An inward view of the Cell obliquely. (detail) 'When you enter the building, whether on foot or horseback and cast your eyes around, upon the yawning ruins, you are struck into an exstatic *reverie*, which none can describe, and they only can be sensible of, that feel it.'

A view of Stonehenge from behind ye high Altar looking towards the grand entrance a little oblique. August 1722. (detail) Stukeley often included druids in his reconstructions of monuments in their original state, but here a druid appears in a naturalistic setting as Stonehenge appeared in the 18th century.

An inward view of Stonehenge or side view of the cell. The figure on the left is sat on the broken Altar Stone. Stukeley considered that in its original form the stone lay flat. The archaeological evidence is inconclusive, but Stukeley may well have been right.

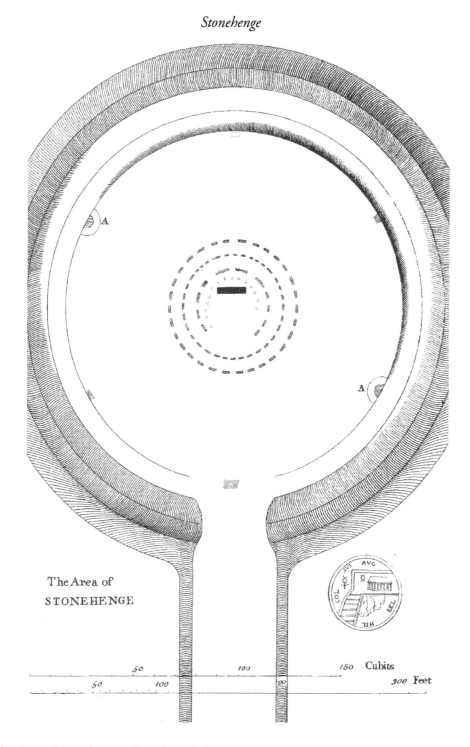

The Area of
STONEHENGE

| | 50 | | 100 | | 150 | Cubits |
| 50 | | 100 | | 200 | | 300 Feet |

The Area of Stonehenge. This plan of the site shows the megalithic monument, the Station Stones, the bank and ditch enclosure, and the start of the previously unnoticed earthwork, the Avenue.

The back prospect of the beginning of the Avenue to Stonehenge. 6 August 1723. Stukeley was the first person to make records of the processional earthwork which ran between Stonehenge and the River Avon some 1.5 miles away. Note the barrow-filled landscape beyond.

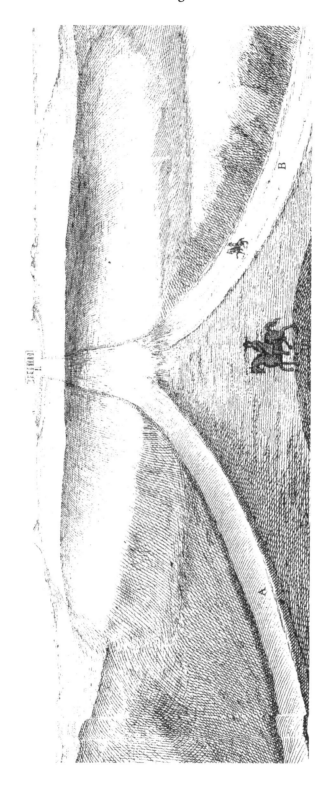

A direct view of Stonehenge from the union of the two Avenues. Stukeley was mistaken in his belief that two avenues led to Stonehenge; the left-hand 'wing' is a true prehistoric avenue, but the other a simple trackway.

Prospect of the west end of the Cursus of Stonehenge. This Late Neolithic earthen processional way or platform was unknown before Stukeley observed it lying half a mile north of Stonehenge in 1723. He named it the 'Cursus' from the Latin for racecourse, suggesting that the 1.75 mile long monument may have been used for chariot races. Since Stukeley's day, many more monuments of the same sort have been discovered throughout Britain, most of them in poor condition, but the name has stuck and 'cursus' now refers to this distinct class of prehistoric site.

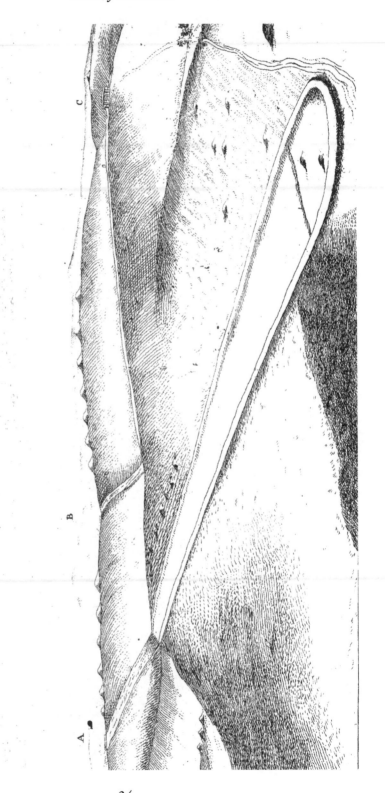

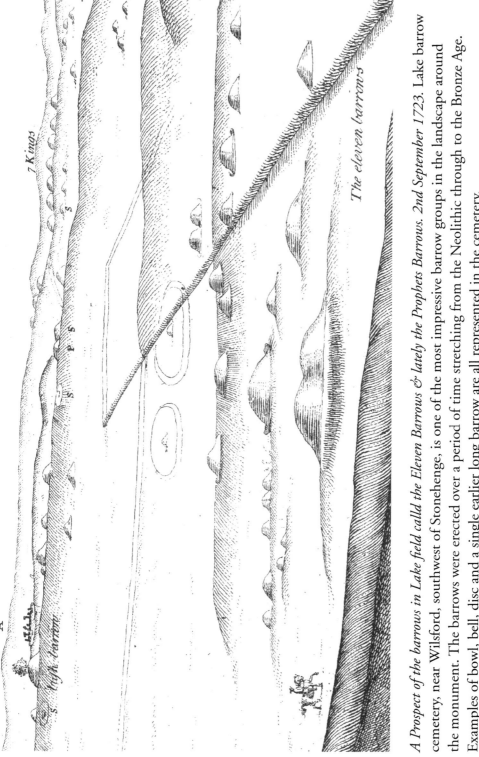

A Prospect of the barrows in Lake field calld the Eleven Barrows & lately the Prophets Barrows. 2nd September 1723. Lake barrow cemetery, near Wilsford, southwest of Stonehenge, is one of the most impressive barrow groups in the landscape around the monument. The barrows were erected over a period of time stretching from the Neolithic through to the Bronze Age. Examples of bowl, bell, disc and a single earlier long barrow are all represented in the cemetery.

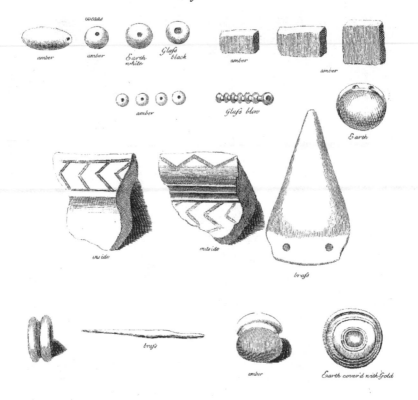

Female Celtic ornaments found in a barrow north of Stonehenge, which I open'd 5 July 1723, among burnt bones, all drawn as big as the Life.

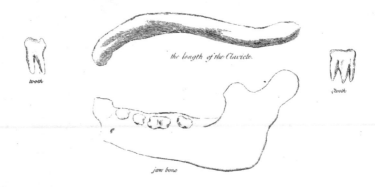

Female Celtic ornaments found in a barrow north of Stonehenge which I opened 5 July 1723, among burnt bones, all drawn as big as the Life. There is no doubt that an inestimable amount of damage was done to prehistoric burial sites during the antiquarian era between 1700 and 1850. No simple treasure hunter, at least Stukeley made records of the artefacts he discovered in the barrows he dug into, which was almost unheard of at the time.

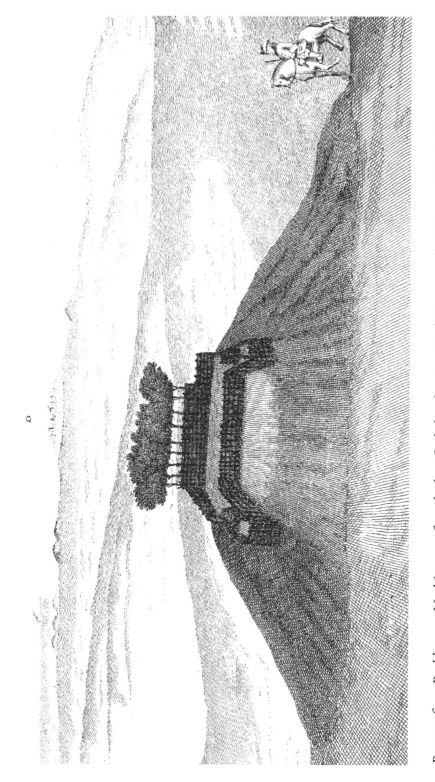

Prospect from Bushbarrow. Nothing was found when Stukeley dug into Bush Barrow, a burial mound in the Normanton Down barrow cemetery southwest of Stonehenge. The barrow was opened by Sir Richard Colt Hoare in 1808, yielding the most spectacular prehistoric artefacts then known in Britain.

Carvilii Regis Tumulus. July 29 1723. A southeast view from this prehistoric barrow, taking in the Iron Age hillfort Old Sarum (B), and the medieval city of Salisbury with the spire of its famous cathedral (C).

Prospect of Stonehenge from the southwest. (*detail*)

A B U R Y,

A

T E M P L E

OF THE

𝕭𝖗𝖎𝖙𝖎𝖘𝖍 𝕯𝕽𝖀𝕵𝕯𝕾,

With Some Others,

D E S C R I B E D.

Wherein is a more particular account of the firſt and patriarchal
religion; and of the peopling the British Islands.

―――― *Quamvis obstet mihi tarda vetustas,*
Multaque me fugiant primis spectata sub annis,
Plura tamen memini ――――   Ov. Met. XII. v. 182.

By *WILLIAM STUKELEY*, M.D.
Rector of *All-Saints* in *Stamford*.

L O N D O N:

Printed for the Author: And Sold by *W. Innys, R. Manby, B. Dod,*
J. Brindley, and the Bookſellers in London.

M DCC XLIII.

3

Avebury

In 1743, three years after *Stonehenge* was finally published, Stukeley's *Abury, A Temple of the British Druids, With Some Others Described* was issued. Even more monumental than *Stonehenge*, *Abury* brought the results of Stukeley's most important fieldwork alongside some of his more esoteric theological musings.

Avebury, a small village that partially encloses the greatest stone circle in the world, lies in North Wiltshire, 17 miles north of Stonehenge. The Avebury landscape, the most monumental aspects of which were constructed throughout the 3rd and 4th millennium BC, is a megalithic wonderland of prehistoric monuments. The main site at Avebury is the largest stone circle in the world, which encloses an area of 28.5 acres and has a diameter of 338 metres, in which stand two smaller, though still massive, stone circles. The megalithic rings of sarsen are enclosed in an enormous roughly circular bank and ditch earthwork. Although dating such a vast monument is notoriously difficult, the outer ring and earthwork is thought to date to the earlier half of the 3rd millennia BC. Two avenues of standing stones once ran to (or from) the main circle; the Kennet Avenue, a good length of which still exists, and the Beckhampton Avenue, almost all traces of which have been destroyed. Each avenue ran for approximately 1.5 miles in length, although the exact location where the Beckhampton Avenue terminates is still to be discovered. Dotted in and around this incredible prehistoric landscape are countless barrows and smaller megalithic sites. The evidence of prehistoric activity is all around, not least of which is Silbury Hill, the mighty earthen mound which stands a mile south of Avebury.

Written references to Stonehenge can be traced back to the 12th century, but widespread knowledge of Avebury came much later. The site was not written about in the context of an ancient place before the middle of the 16th century when John Leland mentioned 'Selberi Hille bottom where by hathe be camps and sepultures.'Wider knowledge of the prodigious prehistoric temple came in 1649 when the antiquary John Aubrey happened upon the place while hunting'. He famously declared that Avebury 'did as much excel Stoneheng, as a Cathedral does a parish church', and prepared the first plans of the monument some years later. While Avebury did, and indeed continues to make Stonehenge look small by comparison, a medieval village had developed in and around the main circles, making the truly monumental scale of the site somewhat difficult to appreciate. Not only that, even at the time of Aubrey's early exploration of the site, many of the individual stones that made up the monument were no longer there. During the 14th and 15th centuries Avebury villagers had dug pits into which they toppled many of the stones, either due to the inconvenience of having to farm around the great megaliths, or perhaps in a superstitious desire to symbolically neutralise the power of this pagan place. If superstition led to the toppling of many of the stones, by the end of the 17th century villagers had more banal intentions. By then people had begun a systematic process of tumbling many of the remaining stones into blazing pits, and pouring cold water onto the heated stones, causing them to shatter when struck. The resulting blocks of manageable sarsen were then used as building material which was incorporated into local buildings. The destruction continued well into the 18th century, a fact which Stukeley lamented but was powerless to stop.

Stukeley came to Avebury in 1719, the first of six extended visits to the area. With place names yet to be standardised through widespread literacy, Stukeley preferred the spelling 'Abury', although his spelling was often inconsistent. He had become aware of the site the previous year when he read a copy of John Aubrey's unpublished notes about ancient sites contained in his chaotic manuscript, the 'Monumenta Britannica'. Even though Aubrey was the first to write at length about Avebury, Stukeley was the first to make accurate records, plans and drawings of the site. Between 1719 and 1724 he explored the Avebury landscape, while all the time villagers were steadily destroying much of what remained of the monument. When the 'miserable havock' finally ended, the temple had been almost totally wrecked. Great arcs of the main circles had gone and a stone circle Stukeley called 'The Sanctuary', which stood at the eastern end of the Kennet Avenue, was no more. Avebury would remain in a ruinous state for years, until millionaire philanthropist Alexander Keiller bought much of the land in and around Avebury village during the 1930s and set into motion a campaign of excavation and reconstruction. In an ironic twist of events, the 14th century villagers who first began the process of burying stones are partly responsible for the improved state of Avebury today. Keiller was able to uncover and re-erect the stones that had been buried in pits, whereas many of the stones that were left untouched in the 1300s and 1400s were toppled and smashed two to three centuries later.

Despite the damage that had taken place by the 18th century, Stukelely saw the monument when it was in reasonably good condition. He was able to record features of the site that would have been surely lost to us if he had not been carrying out fieldwork at the time. Stukeley not only made accounts of Avebury itself, he also carried out fieldwork in the wider Avebury landscape, making records of West Kennet long barrow, Windmill Hill, Silbury Hill, the Devil's Den and the Beckhampton Avenue, among many others.

Abury was not the first book written about Avebury. Thomas Twining's *Avebury in Wiltshire, the remains of a Roman work, erected by Vespatian and Julius Agricola, during their several commands in Britanny,* was published in 1723. While not ranked in the same drawer as Stukeley's *Abury,* Twining did make some interesting observations about Avebury, although he was mistaken about the identity of its builders.

The preface to *Abury* makes Stukeley's post-fieldwork position clear: the Ancient Britons were followers of the original universal religion who raised monuments to the glory of the original Christian God. The obscure theological discussions which dominate the latter part of *Abury* are in sharp contrast to the accounts of his magnificent fieldwork carried out between 1719 and 1724:

'When I first began these studies about the Druid antiquities, I plainly discern'd, the religion profess'd in these places was the first, simple, patriarchal religion… My endeavour in it is to open the times of first planting the world, after the flood; the propagation of true religion together with mankind; the deviation into idolatry; the persons that built the several kinds of patriarchal temples, such as we see here, in the more eastern parts of the world; the planters of Great Britain in particular; and the connexion there is between the east and west in matters of religion. All this shews there was but one religion at first, pure and simple… And our *british* Druids had no images. And whatever we find in history, that looks like idolatry in them, is not to be referr'd to the aboriginal Druids, but to the later colonies from the continent.'

But the later theological intrusions do not detract from the value and importance of *Abury,* which provides an extraordinary account of Avebury as it was in the 18th century, and chronicles aspects of the site and others in the surrounding landscape that we would know a great deal less about without Stukeley's records. Thankfully, most of the fieldwork that Stukeley carried out appeared in *Abury* unadulterated. There were exceptions, the most well known case being Stukeley's deliberate falsification of the appearance of the Sanctuary stone circle in order to support a religious notion (see p. 71). But without question, the good outweighs the bad. Even Stukeley's concept of some stone circles being 'Dracontia' – dragon or serpent temples – resulted in one of the most spectacular and memorable images in *Abury*: 'A Scenographic view of the Druid temple of Abury in north Wiltshire, as in its original'. While it would be convenient for modern observers if *Abury* and *Stonehenge* did not feature Stukeley's more arcane speculations, such a sanitisation of the books would not do justice to the complexity of Stukeley's method of working or to the cultural zeitgeist in which his ideas were formed. *Abury* describes the field-work carried out when Stukeley's brilliance was at its peak, but in the 20 or so years he took to complete the book ready for publication, his concerns had changed markedly.

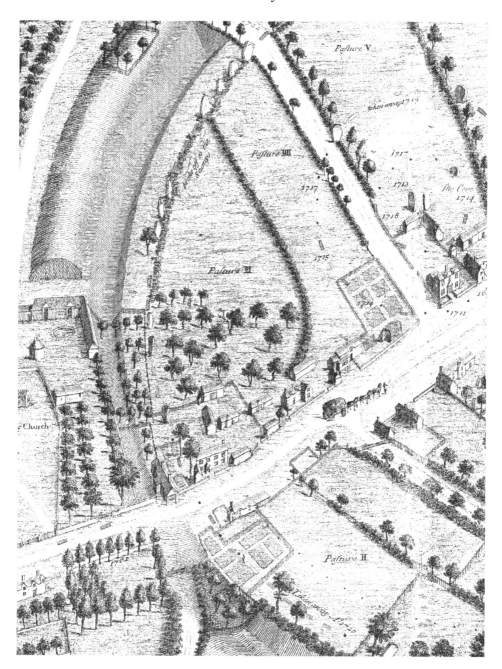

The Groundplot of the Brittish Temple now the town of Aubury Wilts. Anno 1724.
(*detail*) The huge frontispiece to *Abury* showing the condition of Avebury while
Stukeley's fieldwork was underway. The legend indicates stones standing, fallen
and taken away, and also the position of cavities 'visible where a stone stood'. The
detail of Stukeley's survey was unprecedented.

Top: View of the Temple of Rowldrich from the south.

Bottom: View of Rowldrich stones from the West. September 11 1724.

Abury begins with illustrations of the Rollright Stones megalithic complex in Oxfordshire. These engravings show the famous stone circle, the King's Men. The unhewn stones form a ring with a diameter of 33 metres, and the monument is likely to date to the Late Neolithic or Early Bronze Age.

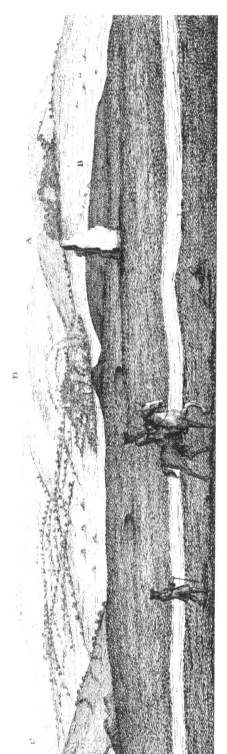

Top: The Prospect Northward from Rowldrich Stones. This engraving shows a standing stone known as the King Stone (A). Stukeley believed the mound (B) beyond the stone was a long barrow; archaeological surveys have shown that it is a natural feature. *Bottom: View of the Kistvaen at Rowldrich from the East.* The Whispering Knights, 400 metres east of the King's Men stone circle, are all that remains of the chamber of a megalithic barrow probably dating to the Neolithic period. Like so many others, the barrow was worn away by ploughing and erosion.

View of the kistvaen of Rowldrich from the south west. A closer view of the Whispering Knights.

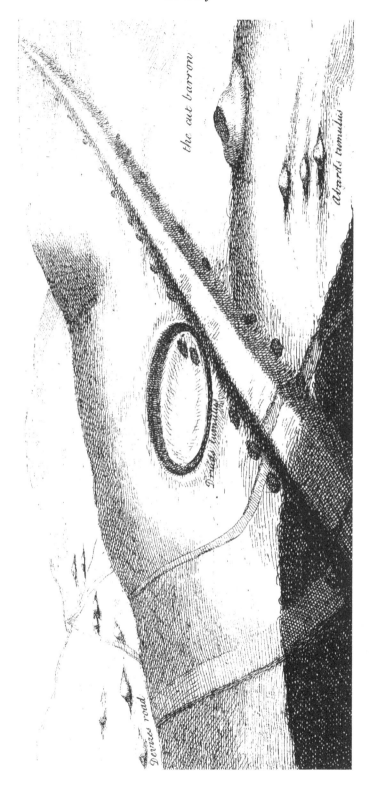

The Roman road leading from Bekampton to Hedington. July 18 1723. Southwest of Avebury, the Beckhampton to Devizes road crosses a Roman road which heads towards Morgan's Hill. Stukeley noted that this Roman road cut through the edge of an earlier prehistoric barrow, as he would also see on Cranborne Chase the following year (see p.17).

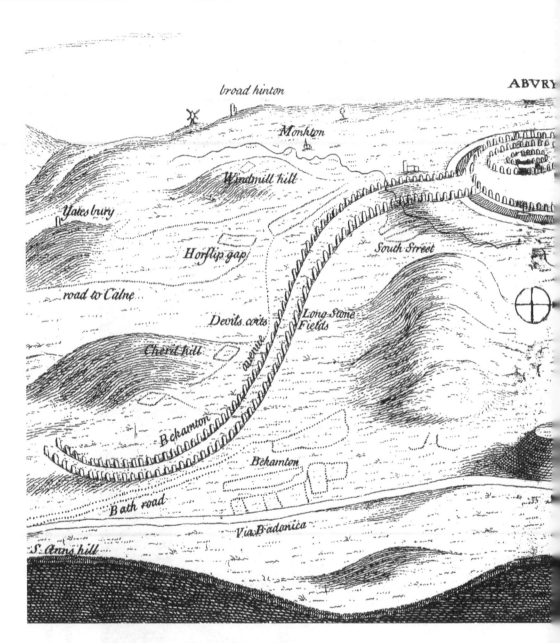

A Scenographic view of the Druid temple at Abury in north Wiltshire as in its original.
This extraordinary interpretation of the Avebury complex is part fieldwork and
part fantasy. Stukeley subtly skews the prehistoric components of the landscape
around Avebury to fit his notions of 'Dracontia', or serpent temples.

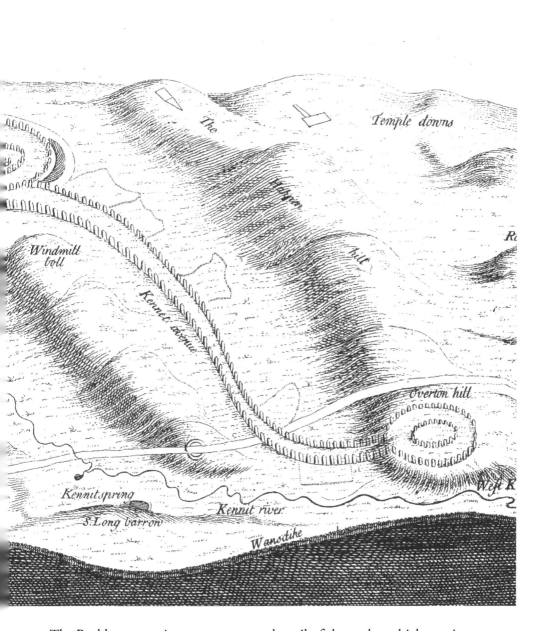

The Beckhampton Avenue represents the tail of the snake, which continues through the main Avebury site, along the West Kennet Avenue to the circle on Overton Hill, which forms the head of the snake.

Rundway hill. 18 July 1723. This engraving shows the view east from Morgan's Hill, east of Roundway Hill, towards the central Marlborough Downs. Oldbury Castle, an Iron Age hillfort on the downs above Calne, is shown along with the Wansdyke, two barrow cemeteries and a medieval enclosure on the right of the picture.

A View of the Remains of the Northern Temple at Abury. August 1722. The main site at Avebury is made up of a huge bank, ditch earthwork and a main stone circle which encloses two further stone circles. The northerly of the two enclosed circles is shown here, already in a ruinous state. Today only two stones remain standing of this once mighty circle, which in its prime had a diameter of almost 100 metres.

Prospect of the Temple on Overton Hill. 8 July 1723. This famous
engraving shows the ruins of the stone and timber circles that stood at
the eastern end of the West Kennet Avenue, which Stukeley popularised
as The Sanctuary. Although the timbers had long since rotted away,
the stone circle existed up until 1723 when a local man, Farmer Green,
removed some stones to the village of West Kennet. The following year

P. 4

Windmill boll

Abury

another man, Farmer Griffin, wrecked what remained. 'This loss of this this work I did not lament alone; but all the neighbours (except the person that gain'd the little dirty profit) were heartily griev'd for it' wrote Stukeley.

Abury

A piece of the great circle, or view at the south entrance into the temple at Abury.
August 1722. The two truly megalithic stones which frame the southern entrance
to Avebury form part of the main outer circle. This engraving illustrates well the
jumble of fields, fences and trees which had grown up in and around the main site
by the 18th century.

Prospect of the Cove Abury. 10 July 1723. Within the northern circle stands a megalithic mystery, the Cove. This box-shaped structure, open to the direction of the midsummer sunrise, is likely to be one of the earliest stone structures at Avebury, and was originally formed by three or perhaps four standing stones. Stukeley coined the term 'cove', which is applied to the dozen or so similar structures known in Britain. Another cove stood on the line of the Beckhampton Avenue to the west of Avebury, although only one stone remains.

The Cove of the Northern temple.

Selin. J.I.

View of the Cell of the Celtic Temple at Abury. August 16 1721. Another view of the Cove, showing how the monument was incorporated into the walls of a much later barn.

Part of the south Temple from the Central Obelisk. 10 July 1723. At the centre of the southern circle stood a solitary, massive 21 feet high megalith. Stukeley reported that this circle was wrecked by farmer John Fowler, and the obelisk soon followed. Today the site is marked by a concrete pillar, and modern druidical rituals are regularly held at this spot.

A View of the South Temple. July 15 1723.

Windmill hill

Bath road

The Entrance of Kennet avenue into Abury. 14 May 1724. The southern entrance to Avebury through the outer earthwork. Windmill Hill, the famous causewayed enclosure 1.5 miles northwest of Avebury, stands on the skyline beyond. This site, made of roughly concentric rings of causewayed ditches, predates the main Avebury complex by about 1,000 years.

'Tom Robinson, another *Herostratus* of the place, made cruel havock among them [the stones]. He own'd to us, that two of them cost eight pounds in the execution.' Stukeley added an unflattering portrait of 'stone-killer' Robinson to *Abury* because of the destruction that he wrought, including taking away an entire section of the stones of the eastern side of the outer circle for building materials. Robinson told Stukeley that it was uneconomical to smash the ancient standing stones, but admitted that he was simply too lazy to fetch untouched sarsens from the nearby downs.

'Reuben [or Ruben] Horsall, parish-clerk, had a due veneration for these sacred remains, and assisted me in the best intelligence he was able to give.' In contrast to Tom Robinson's portrait, the inscription reads 'Ruben Horsall Clark of Abury & Antiquarian. July 29 1722.'

A Prospect from Abury steeple. This view from St. James church looks south past Waden Hill towards Silbury Hill.

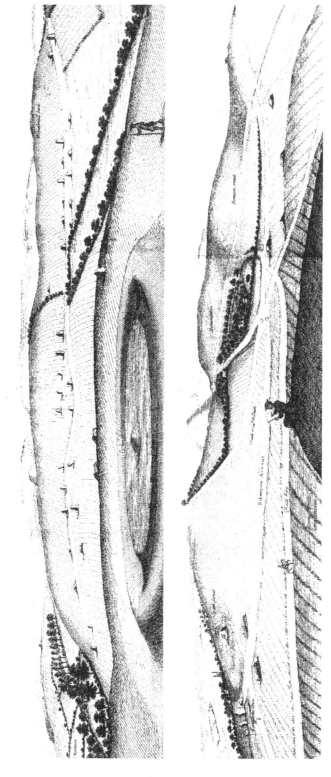

Top: *Prospect of Kennet Avenue from the Druids tumulus on Hakpen Hill. May 15th 1724.*
Bottom: *Prospect of Bekampton Avenue from Longston Long Barrow. 1724.*

A view near the spot of the termination of Bekampton Avenue. July 19 1723. Generations of archaeologists wrote off the existence of Avebury's Beckhampton Avenue, suggesting Stukeley invented the monument to fit his theories about 'dracontia' temples. In 1999 archaeologists confirmed that Stukeley had been right all along when a double row of stone holes spaced 15 metres apart was uncovered. Some stones had been buried, others smashed, and many were missing entirely. Stukeley's description of the Beckhampton Avenue was finally vindicated, 256 years after the publication of *Abury*.

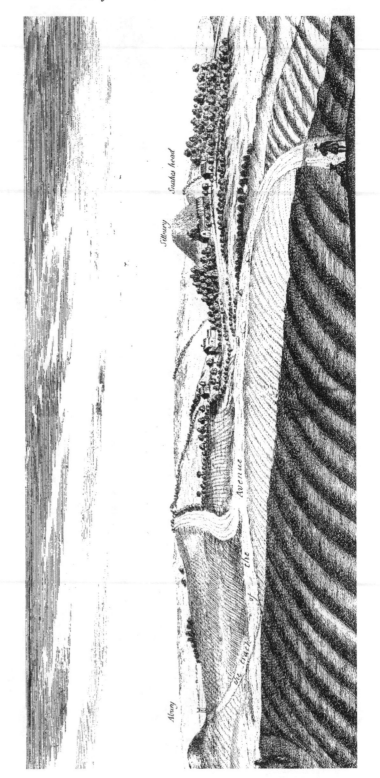

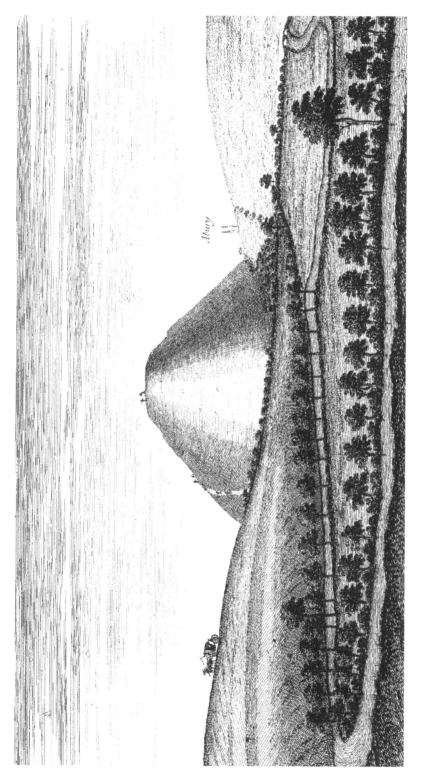

A prospect of Silbury hill from the spring head of the Kennet River. 13 May 1724. A mile south of the Avebury circles stands the incomparable Silbury Hill, a 130 ft tall man-made mound. Its construction has recently been dated to between 2,490 and 2,340 BC. The purpose of this most enigmatic monument is unknown, although there is evidence that a spiral pathway originally led to the summit, suggesting that processions of some sort may have taken place here.

Silbury Hill. July 11 1723. Stukeley observed that a Roman road avoided Silbury by swinging around it; more evidence that these monuments pre-dated the Romans. Scientific techniques mean that many monuments can now be dated accurately, but as recently as the early 1950s some researchers believed that Silbury Hill was a Norman structure.

The HAKPEN or
fnakes head temple on
Overton hill, calld the
Sanctuary.

Avenue

English Feet

The Hakpen or snakes head temple on Overton Hill calld the Sanctuary. This engraving did much to damage Stukeley's reputation because it is clear that he deliberately falsified the shape of the stone circle to support his theory that the site represented the head of a snake. His earlier notes show that Stukeley was aware that the ring of stones was actually a true circle rather than the oval shown here.

71

Top: *A Group of Barrows on the side of the valley above Beckampton.*
Bottom: *A Group of Barrows upon Overton Hill.*
Two examples of Bronze Age linear barrow cemeteries in the Avebury landscape.

Millbarrow in Monkton 215 feet long 55 broad set round with great stones, the broad end Eastward the narrow end West. Mill Barrow chambered long barrow, north of Avebury, was destroyed in the 19th century but the site of the former monument is known.

The Long Barrow South of Silbury Hill. West Kennet long barrow is one of the most famous prehistoric mounds in Britain. The barrow is over 300 ft long and eight ft high, and is thought to have been built during the middle of the 3rd millennia BC. A communal tomb-temple, the barrow was in use until the Early Bronze Age, when a vast blocking stone was placed over its entrance. Reconstructed in the 1950s, today West Kennet long barrow can be visited and its megalithic chambers entered.

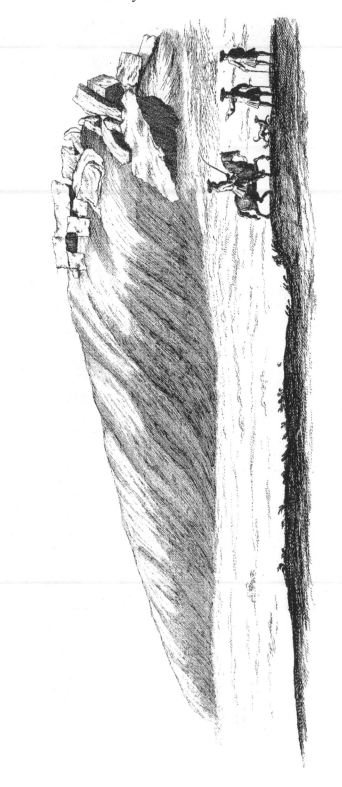

74

Kist Vaen

In Cornwal

In Cornwal

In Monkton field by Abury

Kist Vaen. This engraving illustrates three examples of megalithic burial chambers, all of which would have originally been covered by an earthen mound. The lower image shows a site called the Shelving Stones which stood north of Avebury, but has since been destroyed.

View of the Kist-Vaen in Clatford Bottom. The Devil's Den stands a few miles east of Avebury, several hundred metres north of the road to Marlborough. The stones are the remains of a megalithic chamber at the eastern end of a long barrow. The mound which covered the chamber has been all but obliterated, but a reconstruction of the stones in 1921 means that the megalithic aspects of the site are largely unchanged today.

North-East View of the Kist-Vaen in Clatford Bottom. 1 July 1723.

ITINERARIUM CURIOSUM:

OR,

AN ACCOUNT OF THE

ANTIQUITIES,

AND REMARKABLE

CURIOSITIES

IN

NATURE OR ART,

OBSERVED IN TRAVELS THROUGH

GREAT BRITAIN.

ILLUSTRATED WITH COPPER PLATES.

CENTURIA I.

THE SECOND EDITION,

WITH LARGE ADDITIONS.

By WILLIAM STUKELEY, M. D. F. R. & A. S.

O Patria, O Divûm domus, Albion, inclyta bello !
O quam te memorem, quantum juvat ufque morari
Mirarique tuæ fpeɕacula plurima terræ !

LONDON:

Printed for Meffrs. Baker and Leigh, in York-Street, Covent-Garden.

M.DCC.LXXVI.

4

Itinerarium Curiosum

'The intent of this Treatise is to oblige the curious in the Antiquities of Britain: it is an account of places and things from inspection, not compiled from others' labours, or travels in one's study. I own it is a work crude and hasty, like the notes of a traveller that stays not long in a place; and such it was in reality. Many matters I threw in only as hints for further scrutiny, and memorandums for myself or others: above all, I avoided prejudice, never carrying any author along with me, but taking things in the natural order and manner they presented themselves: and if my sentiments of Roman stations, and other matters, happen not to coincide with what has been wrote before me; it was not that I differ from them, but things did not so appear to me. The prints, beside their use in illustrating the discourses, are ranged in such a manner as to become an index of enquiries for those that travel, or for a British Antiquary. I shall probably continue this method at reasonable intervals. The whole is to invite Gentlemen and others in the country, to make researches of this nature, and to acquaint the world with them: they may be assured, that whatever accounts of this sort they please to communicate to me, they shall be applied to proper use, and all due honour paid to the names of those that favour me with a correspondence so much to the glory and benefit of our country, which is my sole aim therein.'

From the preface to Stukeley's *Itinerarium Curiosum*.

Itinerarium Curiosum, Or, An Account of the Antiquitys and Remarkable Curiositys in Nature and Art, Observ'd in Travels thro' Great Britain, published in 1724, and again in a greatly expanded version of 1776, detailed Stukeley's series of tours around Britain carried out during the 1710s. Monuments of every sort interested him, from Roman to medieval crosses, to natural 'wonders' of nature.

While an interesting topo- graphical work in its own right, Stukeley's earlier tours did not take in many prehis- toric sites. Stukeley's interest in pre-

Roman Britain was still developing during the 1710s, and the book has none of the systematic fieldwork of *Stonehenge* or *Abury*. Still, Stukeley was already an excellent draughtsman and the *Itinerarium Curiosum* contains much to enjoy. The second edition of 1776 brought together a wealth of previously unpublished material, and it is from this version that the following engravings are reproduced. A two volume facsimile edition was published by Gregg International Publishers Limited, of Farnborough, Hampshire in 1969.

The tone of the frontispiece to the *Itinerarium Curiosum* reflects Stukeley's early interest in the classical world, and Roman Britain in particular.

This portrayal of an imaginary Roman bust of 'William Stukeley Medical Doctor'
contrasts with the frontispiece to *Stonehenge* (p.13), which shows a greater
druidical influence.

Top: *Marlborough Mount.*
Bottom: *Cascade at Wilton.* Stukeley often stayed at the home of his antiquarian
friend and colleague Lord Pembroke at Wilton, South Wiltshire during his
fieldwork of the 1720s. This engraving is 'Dedicated to the Right Honorable the
Lady Hartford', wife of Stukeley's colleague Lord Hartford.

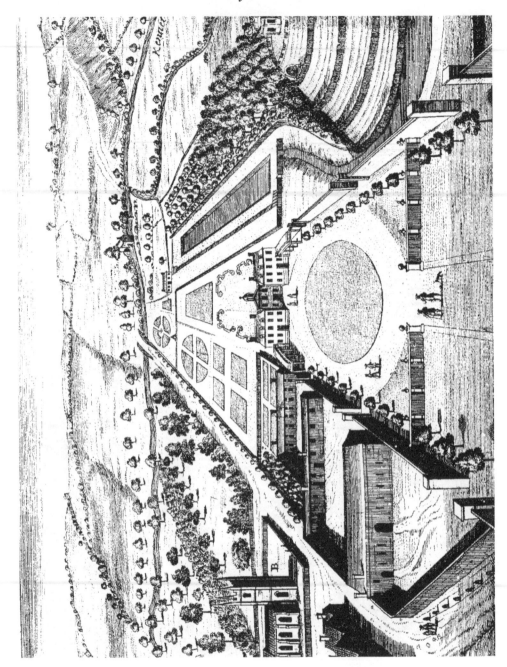

*View of Lord Hartford's House at Marlborough. 29 June 1723. Marlborough lies
five miles east of Avebury.* The Marlborough Mound, illustrated here, looks like a
smaller version of Silbury Hill, and until very recently was thought to be a medieval
structure. However, in 2011 archeologists discovered that like Silbury, the mound's
origins were prehistoric.

The West View of Waltham in Jul. 1721

Petro Le Neve Ar.
Norroy. tab. d. d.
W. Stukeley.

Stukeley delin.

The West View of Waltham Cross. 11 July 1721. This medieval cross at Waltham, Essex, was erected in 1290 on the course of the funeral procession of Queen Eleanor, wife of King Edward I, when her body was transported from Lincolnshire to London.

A Prospect of the British Cursus near Leicester, call'd Raw Dikes from the hills above. September 10 1722. Stukeley misidentified this earthwork as a prehistoric cursus; Raw Dykes are in fact the remains of a Roman canal.

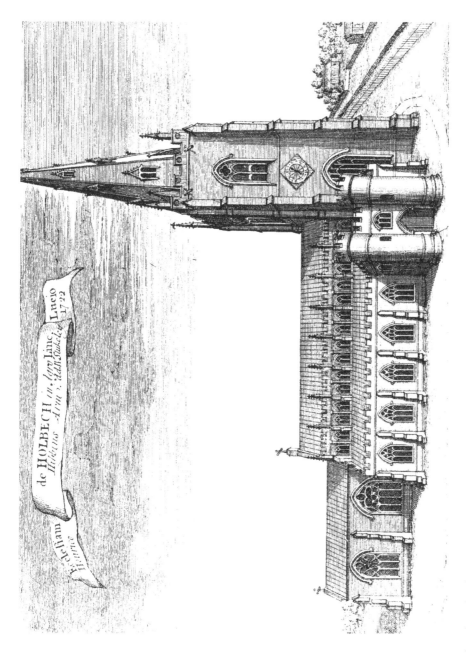

Holbeach Church, drawn in 1722. Stukeley was born in the market town of Holbeach, Lincolnshire in 1687, and lived there until he went to Cambridge in 1703.

The high Altar at St. Albans. 28 December 1720. England's first Christian martyr, Alban, was beheaded by the Romans here around 300 AD. The site has been hallowed ever since.

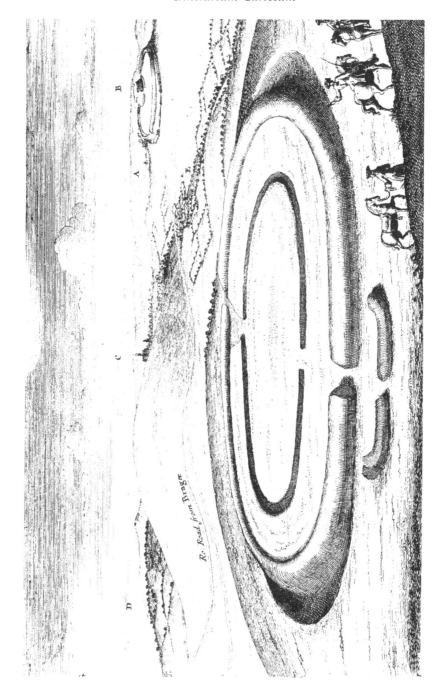

Figsbury Rings, South Wiltshire, drawn August 25, 1723. This enigmatic earthwork stands on high ground east of Salisbury. The outer ditch and bank is Iron Age, but encloses an inner ditch which is likely to be a much earlier henge or causewayed enclosure.

The Prospect of Glasenbury Abby. Glastonbury, in Somerset, is said to be where Joseph of Arimathea built the first Christian church in England. The town's association with King Arthur also ensures that pilgrims of many kinds still travel to the town each year.

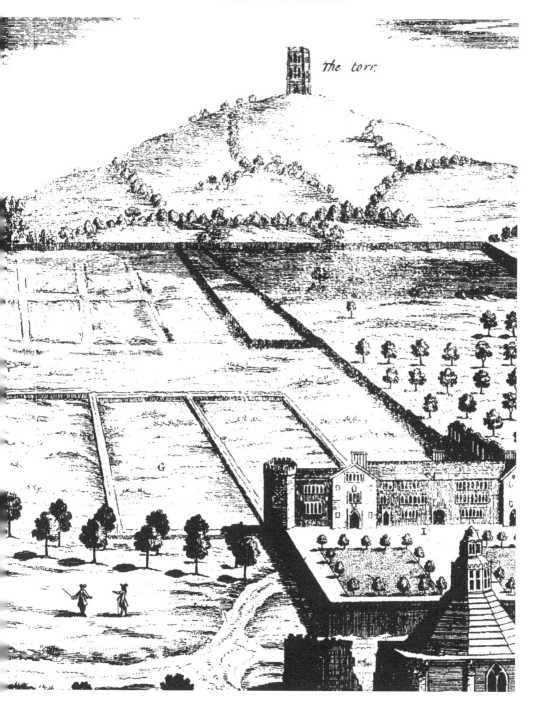

the torr.

G

I

Oldbury Castle. 11 July 1723. The northern escarpment of this Iron Age hillfort, also shown on p.54, is now flanked by the Cherhill White Horse hill-figure which was cut in 1780.

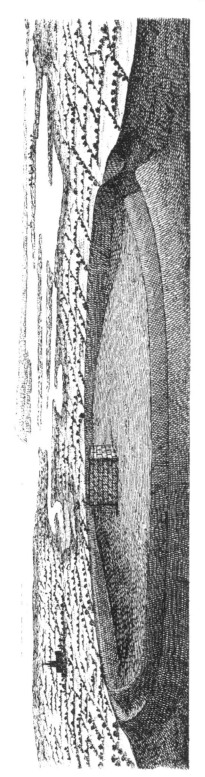

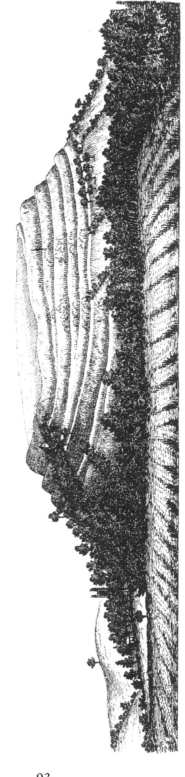

Top: *Prospect from St. Roc's Hill. September 15 1723.*
The Trundle causewayed enclosure and later hillfort on St Roches Hill, West Sussex.

Bottom: *Prospect of Camalet Castle. 15 August 1723.*
South Cadbury Castle, Somerset, has been occupied through the Neolithic, Bronze Age, Iron Age, Roman, Sub-Roman and Medieval periods. Extensive Iron Age earthwork defences are the most striking aspects of the site.

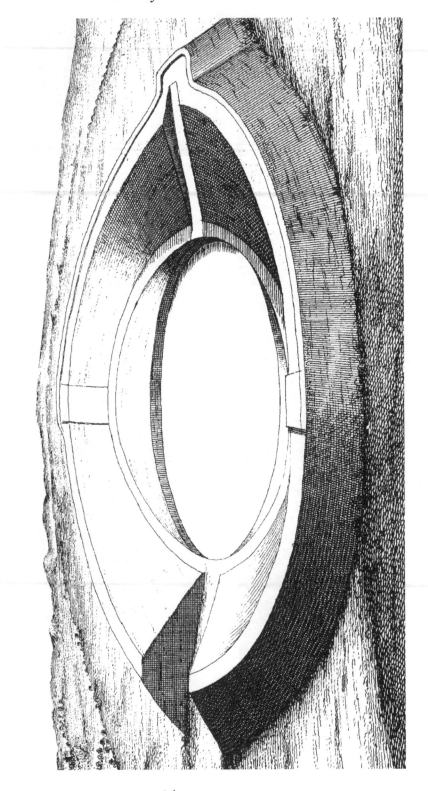

The Side View of Dorchester Amphitheater. Archological excavation of this Dorset earthwork, called Maumbury Rings, has shown that before it was put to use as a Roman amphitheatre it was a Neolithic henge monument about 85 metres in diameter. Stukeley's 1723 paper about this site was the first archaeological text he published.

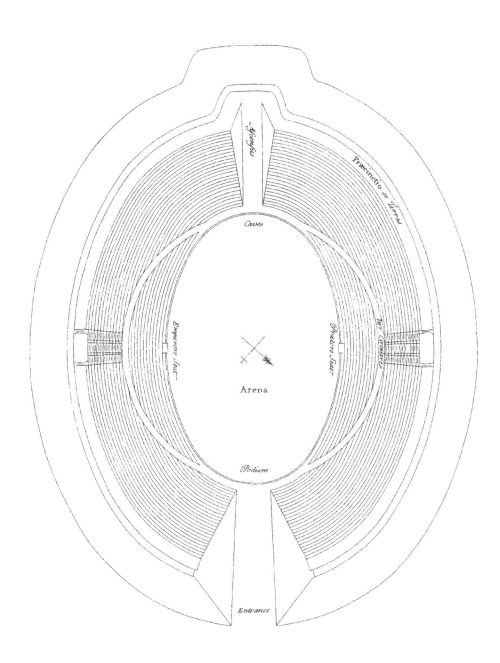

The Geometrical Groundplot of the Roman Amphitheatre at Dorchester. August 22 1723.

This engraved map of Roman roads in Britain, drawn by Stukeley in 1723, records his 'iters', or tours, throughout the country.

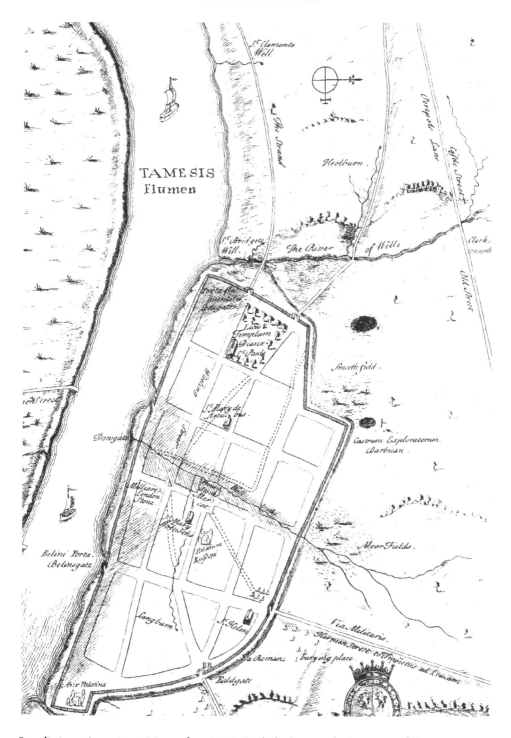

Londinium Augusia. 7 November 1722. Stukeley's speculative map of Roman
London, the centre of Roman power in Britain.

Aquae Solis. July 21, 1723. From the top of the Southern Hill. The great Georgian city of Bath has been fashionable since the 18th century, when people would come to take the medicinal spring waters after which the city is named. Bath's history stretches back at least to Roman times, and extensive Roman remains can still be visited here.

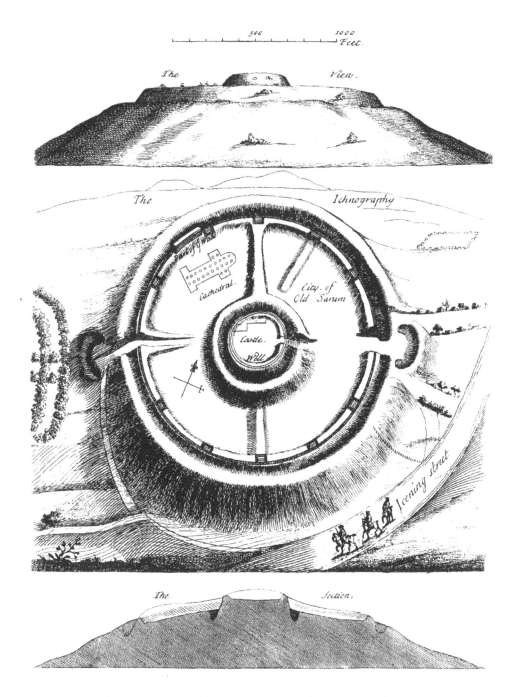

Sorbiodunum. 1 August 1723. Old Sarum, north of Salisbury, originated as an impressive Iron Age hillfort. It was later settled by the Romans, and much later a Norman castle motte was added. The foundations of an 11th century cathedral, castle and bishop's palace lie within the hillfort.

Prospect of Old Sarum. August 1 1723.

Prospect of Lyme. 21 August 1723. Stukeley's tours did not take him much further west than Lyme Regis, in Dorset. This engraving of the view east across Lyme Bay shows the Isle of Portland further along the coast (B). Stukeley suggested that prehistoric travellers may have arrived from mainland Europe at Portland.

A Prospect of Ad Pontem upon the Eminence, A Mile South on the Fosse. September 7 1722. Ad Pontem, 'the place of the bridges', is the site of a Roman fort and town on the Fosse Way, East Stoke, Thorpe by Newark, Nottinghamshire.

2. 2ᵈ

Holbech Cross   *Lincolnshire*

*Ob amorem erga Solum Natale, Temporum
Ignorantia direptum restituit Wᵐˢ Stukeley 1722.*

Holbech Cross Lincolnshire. A Medieval cross in Stukeley's home town of Holbeach.

ADVERTISEMENT.

THAT Dr. Stukeley had altered the plan of his intended Hiftory of the antient Celts, &c. mentioned in the Preface of the former part of this work, plainly appears by his publifhing *Stonehenge* and *Abury* feparately: but, as many of the Plates he left unpub-lifhed were undoubtedly intended for that Work, and others for a Second Volume of the *Itinerarium*, neither of which were ever completed; the Editor hopes it will give pleafure to the Learned to fee thofe Plates, together with fuch of his Tracts as relate to them, collected into one Volume, and that they will be found not altogether unworthy of their attention;—fenfible however that the many defects which muft unavoidably happen in publifhing a Pofthumous Collection from loofe papers, and notes carelefsly thrown together, will ftand in need of their candid indulgence.

The Itinerary of Richard of Cirencefter, together with Dr. Stukeley's Account of, and Obfervations upon it, were thought by fome Friends of the Doctor a very proper addition. It is a tract truly valuable for the new light it has thrown on the ftudy of Britifh Antiquities, and being out of print is now become very fcarce.

It may be expected that fome account fhould in this place be given of the Author, and his Works. A Catalogue of thofe which have appeared in print we fubjoin; and for his Life we refer the reader to Mr. Mafters's Hiftory of Benet College, Cambridge, printed in quarto, 1753; adding only, that he died March 3d, 1765, in his 78th year, and was buried in the church-yard of Eaft-Ham in Effex, having ordered by his will that no memorial of him fhould be erected there.

This notice appeared in Part II of the 1776 edition of Stukeley's *Itinerarium Curiosum*.

Prospect of Burrow hill from the Leicester road. September 8 1722. A view of Burrough-on-the Hill Iron Age hillfort in Leicestershire, a county with few monumental prehistoric sites.

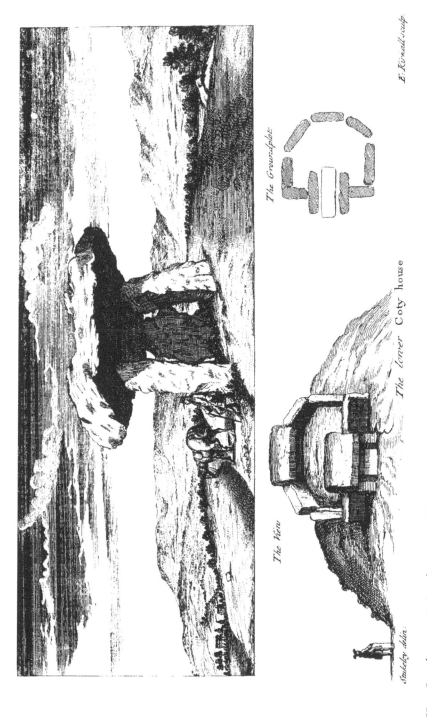

The Groundplot.

E. Kirkall sculp.

The View

The lower Coty house

Stukeley delin:

Top: *Kits Coty house. 15 October 1722. N.E. Prospect.* Bottom: *The Lower Coty house.* Like the Devil's Den in Wiltshire (p.77), the stones of Kit's Coty House in Kent is the megalithic remains of a chambered long barrow. Lower Kit's Coty House, or the Countless Stones, are now a jumble of loose sarsens, but Stukeley's engraving shows the reconstructed site in the form of the remains of a chambered long barrow. Compare with the illustration on p.111.

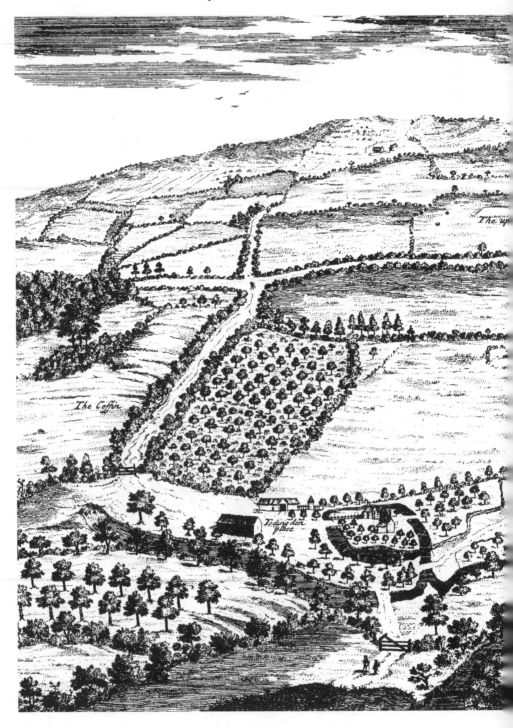

A prospect of the Country from Kits Coty house. October 15 1722. The Countless Stones are shown in the middle of the right-hand page.

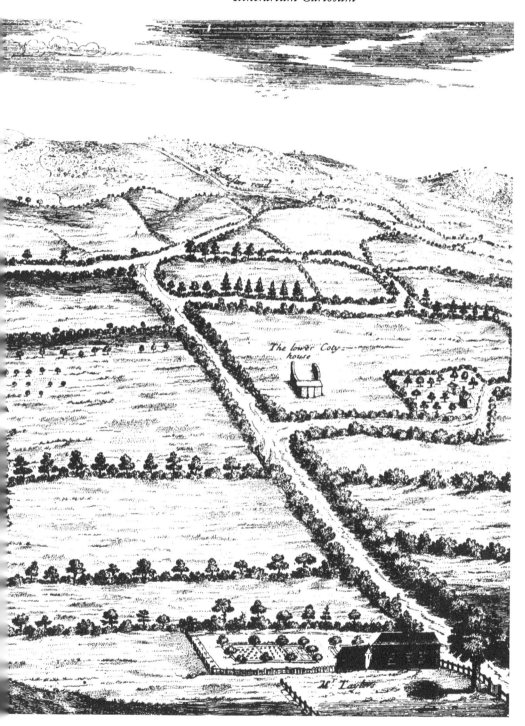

A prospect of Kits Coty House Kent. October 15 1722. The mound of the long barrow, much reduced in Stukeley's day, has been almost obliterated by ploughing and erosion.

View of the Ruins of the Lower Coty house. A closer view of the Countless Stones.

The side view of Caesars bridge. An imaginative illustration of Caesar's famous bridge over the Rhine, which his army is supposed to have built in only 10 days.

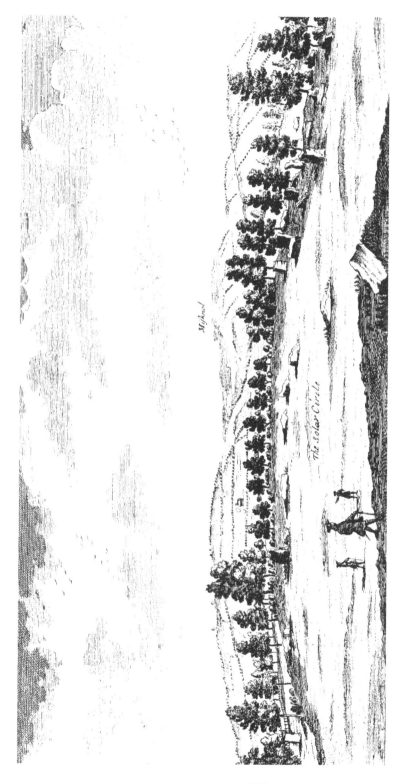

A View of Stanton Drew. 23 July 1723. After Avebury and Stonehenge, Stanton Drew, six miles south of Bristol, is the most important megalithic complex in Wessex. The group contains three stone circles, two stone avenues and a cove. The largest ring, the Great Circle, has a diameter of 375 feet; only the main circle at Avebury is larger. The two smaller circles are approximately 140 and 100 feet across. The largest and smallest circles both have megalithic avenues attached that lead to the River Chew, which runs nearby. Despite the state of ruination which the monuments are in, Stanton Drew is well worth visiting.

The Cove at Stanton Drew. In the garden of the Druid's Arms pub in Stanton Drew stands the Cove. The monument is made up of two megaliths with a recumbent slab between the two, and is aligned with the centres of the largest and smallest stone circles of the complex.

A View at Stanton Drew.

The Celtic Temple *at*
Claſserneſs in the Iſle
of Lewis in Scotland.

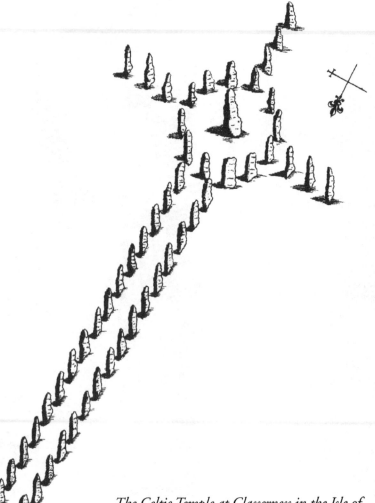

*The Celtic Temple at Classerness in the Isle of
Lewis in Scotland.* Stukeley based his drawing
of the magnificent Callanish stone circle in the
Outer Hebrides from a drawing by Edward
Lhuyd, which was itself copied from an earlier
drawing by Martin Martin.

116

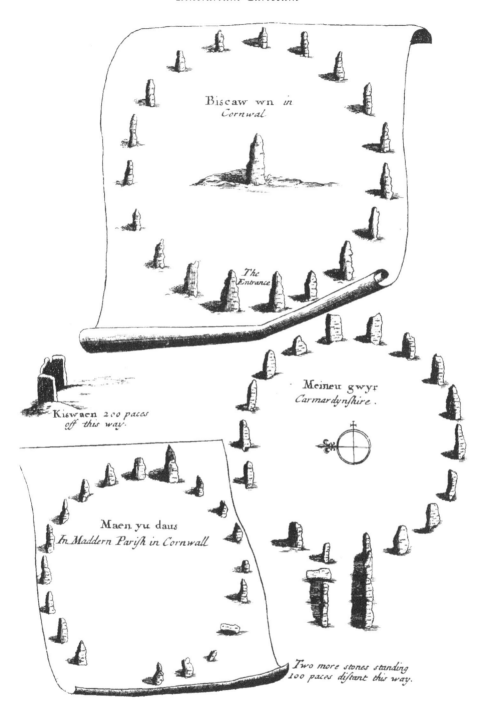

Celtic Temples. This engraving shows three stone circles, 'Biscaw wn in Cornwall' (Boscawen-Un, Cornwall), 'Meineu gwyr' (Meini-gwyr, Carmarthenshire) and 'Maen yu daus In Maddern Parish in Cornwall' (the Merry Maidens, Cornwall).

A Celtic Temple at Winterburn. 22 August 1723. The Nine Stones stone circle, Winterbourne Abbas, is one of a small group of ruinous Dorset rings. Stukeley's illustration shows a track running alongside the circle; today, the busy A35 Dorchester to Bridport road thunders past this impressive little site.

Celtic Monuments in Germany. As antiquarianism spread throughout Europe, information about prehistoric sites in other countries began to circulate. Like the sites in Cornwall, Scotland and Ireland included in the *Itinerarium Curiosum*, Stukeley would not have seen these overseas monuments in the field.

Irish sites: Lough Gur, County Limerick (left) and Newgrange, County Meath (right). 'The Mount of New Grange in the County of East Meath not far from Drogheda. There are 4 other Mounts near this, 3 lesser & the 4th as big as this.'

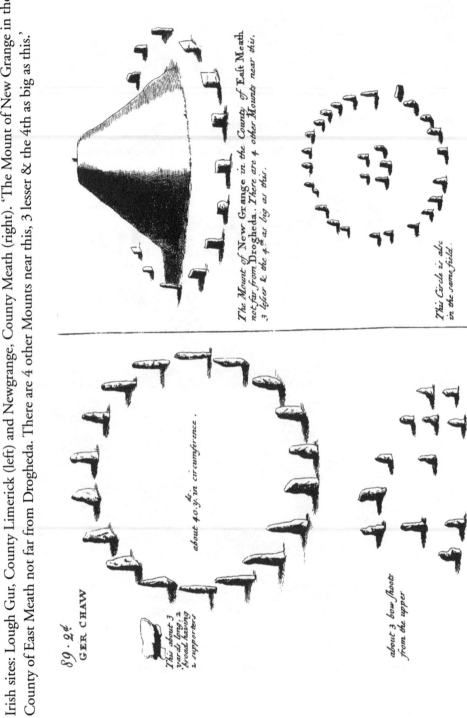

The Mount of New Grange in the County of East Meath not far from Drogheda. There are 4 other Mounts near this, 3 lesser & the 4.th as big as this.

This Circle is also in the same feild.

89.2¢
GER CHAW

This about 3 yards long, 2 broad, having 2 supporters

about 40.y. in circumference.

about 3 bow shoots from the upper

The great Temple & Grave of the Druids at Trerdrew in Anglesey. Stukeley based his reconstruction of the Bryn Gwyn Stones on a sketch by the Rev. Henry Rowlands, published in his Mona Antiqua Restaurata (1723). The site, whatever form it really took, has been ruined and only two stones remain

The Devils Arrows near Burrowbridg. 14 September 1725. The Devil's Arrows near Boroughbridge, North Yorkshire are three standing stones, the tallest of which is almost 23 feet high, arranged in an almost straight line. It is likely that the monument was originally made up of five stones rather than the three which remain.

Postscript

Stukeley's 18th century investigation of ancient sites was founded on early anti-quarian work carried out the previous century, but the detailed records that he made about monuments and their relationship with the wider landscapes in which they stood were without precedent. The methodology of his rigorous fieldwork was quite unlike anything that had come before, and paved the way for the scientific study of archaeology which evolved from the 19th century to the present. At the same time, Stukeley's esoteric theories about ancient Britain inspired members of the druidical revival of the 19th century, itself allied to the romantic movement that flourished in the arts during the same period. While the modern archaeological establishment has tended to underplay the importance of Stukeley and his fellow antiquarians, artists, writers, poets and others enthralled by the romance of Ancient Albion have been less reluctant to acknowledge the influence of the Arch-Druid Chyndonax.

The influence of Stukeley's books on William Blake (1757–1827) is well established. Both Stuart Piggott (in his two Stukeley biographies) and John Michell (in *Megalithomania*) have detailed the allusions to *Stonehenge* and *Abury* in Blake's illuminated books, *Milton* and *Jerusalem*. John Michell has referred to the difference between Blake and Stukeley as being that of a 'poet and priest'. For Stukeley, the builders of Stonehenge and Avebury were wise holy men carrying out God's original will; to Blake, the megalithic monuments symbolised humanity's fall from divine innocence into a state of moralistic religious bondage.

In the stuffy archaeological literature of the 19th century, Stukeley's influence can still be felt; in Sir Richard Colt Hoare's *The Ancient History of Wiltshire I & II* (1810–1821) and Reverend A. C. Smith's *Guide to British and Roman Antiquities of the North Wiltshire Downs* (1884 and 1885). Heywood's Sumner's illustrations in *The Ancient Earthworks of Cranborne Chase* (1913) clearly drew on Stukeley's books, showing archaeological monuments within naturalistic, Arts and Crafts movement-inspired landscapes. There is more than a little Stukeley in Sumner's illustrations for Frank Stevens' *Stonehenge Today & Yesterday* (1933).

More recently, Aubrey Burl, the world's most respected authority on megalithic monuments, dedicated *Prehistoric Avebury* (1979 and 2002) to Stukeley. Our hero makes an unexpected appearance in John Fowles' *A Maggot* (1995), in which a character learns about Stonehenge 'not by the black arts' but by a meeting with 'the Reverend William Stukeley of Stamford, the antiquary... his drawings and choreographies... just and worthy of attention'. Images of or by Stukeley have appeared on the covers of books (Rodney Legg's *Stanton Drew: The Great Western Temple*, 1998), magazines (*Avebury Henge Almanac 1*, February 1998), programmes (Megalithomania! Conference 2002), postcards, badges and T-shirts. And could any lover of British Antiquities fail to be impressed by the name of Holbeach's William Stukeley Church of England Primary School?

Ultimately, the impact of Stukeley's work has been two-fold. Firstly, his pioneering fieldwork carried out at Stonehenge and Avebury was a crucial stepping stone in the development of modern archaeology. Secondly, Stukeley's love of the antiquities and landscapes of Britain, and the feeling that the ancient past could be grasped – if only in fragments – was so strong that his greatest work still has the power to charm, inspire and inform almost three hundred years later:

'The strolling for relaxed minds upon these downs is the most agreeable exercise and amusement in the world especially when you are every minute struck with some piece of wonder in antiquity. The neat turn of the huge barrow wraps you up into a contemplation of the flux of life and passage from one state to another and you meditate with yourself on the fate and fortune of the famous personages who thus took care of their ashes that have rested so many ages.'

The next four pages show examples of plates from two of William Blake's illuminated books which were clearly influenced by Stukeley's work. The first is from *Milton: a poem* (1804), and the second and third are from *Jerusalem: The Emanation of the Giant Albion* (1804). Compare the final image of *Jerusalem* (p.128–9) with *Abury's* 'Scenographic Plan' (p.50–51) of the previous century, in which Blake brings together the trilithons of *Stonehenge* with *Abury's* serpent temples, in a potent and iconic image of prehistoric Britain.

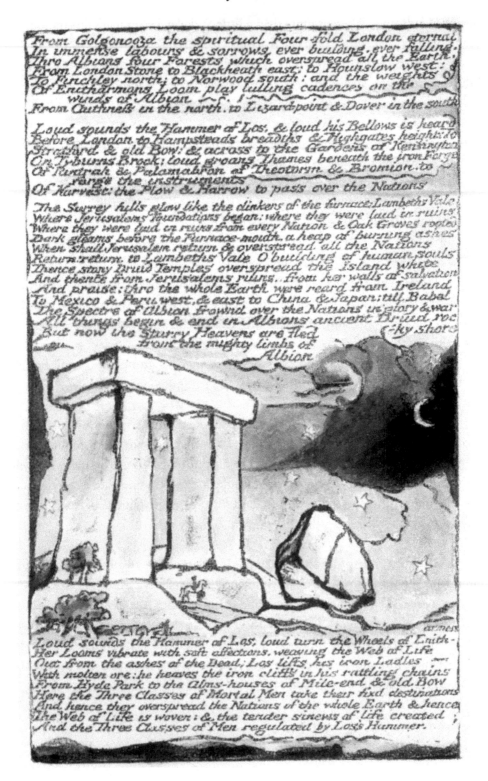

From Golgonooza the spiritual Four fold London eternal
In immense labours & sorrows, ever building, ever falling:
Thro Albions four Forests which overspread all the Earth:
From London Stone to Blackheath east: to Hounslow west:
To Finchley north: to Norwood south: and the weights of
Of Enitharmons Loom play lulling cadences on the
     winds of Albion
From Cathness in the north, to Lizardpoint & Dover in the south

Loud sounds the Hammer of Los, & loud his Bellows is heard
Before London to Hampsteads breadths & Highgates heights: To
Stratford & old Bow: & across to the Gardens of Kensington
On Tyburns Brook: loud groans Thames beneath the iron Forge
Of Rintrah & Palamabron of Theotorm & Bromion to
     range the instruments
Of Harvest: the Plow & Harrow to pass over the Nations

The Surrey hills glow like the clinkers of the furnace: Lambeths Vale
Where Jerusalems foundations began: where they were laid in ruins
Where they were laid in ruins from every Nation & Oak Groves rooted
Dark gleams before the Furnace-mouth, a heap of burning ashes
When shall Jerusalem return & overspread all the Nations
Return: return to Lambeths Vale O building of human souls
Thence stony Druid Temples overspread the Island white
And thence from Jerusalems ruins, from her walls of salvation
And praise: thro the whole Earth were reard, from Ireland
To Mexico & Peru west, & east to China & Japan: till Babel
The Spectre of Albion frownd over the Nations in glory & war
All things begin & end in Albions ancient Druid rocky shore
But now the Starry Heavens are fled
     from the mighty limbs of
          Albion

Loud sounds the Hammer of Los, loud turn the Wheels of Enith-
Her Looms vibrate with soft affections, weaving the Web of Life
Out from the ashes of the Dead; Los lifts his iron Ladles
With molten ore: he heaves the iron cliffs in his rattling chains
From Hyde Park to the Alms-houses of Mile-end & old Bow
Here the Three Classes of Mortal Men take their fixd destinations
And hence they overspread the Nations of the whole Earth & hence
The Web of Life is woven: &, the tender sinews of life created
And the Three Classes of Men regulated by Los's Hammer.

And this the form of mighty Hand sitting on Albions cliffs
Before the face of Albion: a mighty threatning Form.

His bosom wide & shoulders huge overspreading wondrous
Bear Three strong sinewy Necks & Three awful & terrible Heads
Three Brains in contradictory council brooding incessantly,
Neither daring to put in act its councils, fearing each other.
Therefore rejecting Ideas as nothing & holding all Wisdom
To consist in the agreements & disagreements of Ideas.
Plotting to devour Albions Body of Humanity & Love.

Such Form the aggregate of the Twelve Sons of Albion took; & such
Their appearance when combind; but often by birth pangs & loud groans
They divide to Twelve: the key-bones & the chest dividing in pain
Disclose a hideous orifice; thence issuing the Giant-brood
Arise as the smoke of the furnace, shaking the rocks from sea to sea.
And there they combine into Three Forms, named Bacon & Newton & Locke.
In the Oak Groves of Albion which overspread all the Earth.

Imputing Sin & Righteousness to Individuals: Rahab
Sit deep within him hid: his Feminine Power unreveald
Brooding Abstract Philosophy, to destroy Imagination, the Divine-
Humanity A Three-fold Wonder: feminine: most beautiful: Three-fold
Each within other. On her white marble & even Neck, her Heart
Inorbd and bonified: with locks of shadowing modesty, shining
Over her beautiful Female features, soft flourishing in beauty
Beams mild, all love and all perfection, that when the lips
Recieve a kiss from Gods or Men, a threefold kiss returns
From the press'd loveliness: so her whole immortal form three-fold
Three-fold embrace returns: consuming lives of Gods & Men
In fires of beauty melting them as gold & silver in the furnace
Her Brain enlabyrinths the whole heaven of her bosom & loins
To put in act what her Heart wills: O who can withstand her power
Her name is Vala in Eternity: in Time her name is Rahab

The Starry Heavens all were fled from the mighty limbs of Albion His

129

William Stukeley Bibliography

Of the Roman Amphitheatre at Dorset, 1723 (reprinted for the Quatuor Coronati Lodge of Freemasons in 1925).

Itinerarium Curiosum, Or, An Account of the Antiquitys and Remarkable Curiositys in Nature or Art, Observ'd in Travels thro' Great Brittan, 1724.

Stonehenge: A Temple Restor'd to the British Druids, 1740 (reprinted in 1848 and again in 1982 by Garland Publishing).

Abury: A Temple of the British Druids, 1743 (reprinted in 1848 and again in 1982 by Garland Publishing).

An Account of Richard of Cirencester, Monk of Westminster, and of his Works: With his Antient Map of Roman Britain; And the Itinerary Thereof, 1757.

Itinerarium Curiosum, Or, An Account of the Antiquitys and Remarkable Curiositys in Nature or Art, Observ'd in Travels thro' Great Brittan, 1776 (revised two volume edition, reprinted by Gregg International Publishers in 1969).

The Family Memoirs of the Rev. William Stukeley and the Antiquarian and Other Correspondence of William Stukeley, Roger *& Samuel Gale, etc*, 1882, 1883 and 1887 (three volumes edited by W. C. Lukis for the Surtees Society).

The Commentarys, Diary, and Common-Place Book of William Stukeley, Doppler Press, 1980.

Stonehenge: The unpublished manuscript of The History of the Temples and Religion of the Antient Celts, Part II, 1721–24, 2004 (Yale University Press, eds. Aubrey Burl and Neil Mortimer).

Note: This bibliography includes only those publications directly relevant to *Stukeley Illustrated*. An extensive bibliography of Stukeley's books and manuscripts may be found in David Boyd Haycock's *William Stukeley: Science, Religion and Archaeology in Eighteenth-Century England*.

Further Reading

William Stukeley:

David Boyd Haycock, *William Stukeley: Science, Religion and Archaeology in Eighteenth-Century England*, The Boydell Press, 2002.

David Boyd Haycock, 'The Questionable Reputation of Dr William Stukeley', *3rd Stone 45*: 16–21, 2002.

Stuart Piggott, *William Stukeley: An Eighteenth-Century Antiquary*, Oxford University Press, 1950.

Stuart Piggott, *William Stukeley: An Eighteenth-Century Antiquary (Revised and Enlarged Edition)*, Thames and Hudson, 1985.

Stuart Piggott (ed.), *Sale Catalogues of Libraries of Eminent Persons, Vol 10: Antiquaries*, Mansell, 1974.

Antiquarianism:

Paul G. Bahn, *The Cambridge Illustrated History of Archaeology*, Cambridge University Press, 1996.

Michael Hunter, *John Aubrey and the Realm of Learning*, Duckworth, 1975.

Barry M. Marsden, *The Early Barrow Diggers*, Tempus Publishing, 1999.

Stan A. E. Mendyk, *Speculum Britanniae: Regional Study, Antiquarianism, and Science in Britain to 1700*, University of Toronto Press, 1989.

John Michell, *Megalithomania: Artists, Antiquarians and Archaeologists at the Old Stone Monuments*, Thames and Hudson, 1982.

Graham Parry, *The Trophies of Time: English Antiquarians of the Seventeenth Century*, Oxford University Press, 1995.

Stuart Piggott, *Ruins in a Landscape: Essays in Antiquarianism*, Edinburgh University Press, 1976.

Stuart Piggott, *Antiquity Depicted: Aspects of Archaeological Illustration*, Thames and Hudson, 1978.

Stuart Piggott, *Ancient Britons and the Antiquarian Imagination*, Thames and Hudson, 1989.

Alain Schnapp, *The Discovery of the Past*, British Museum Press, 1996.

Sam Smiles, *The Image of Antiquity: Ancient Britain and the Romantic Imagination*, Yale University Press, 1994.

Stonehenge:

Aubrey Burl, *The Stonehenge People: Life and Death at the World's Greatest Stone Circle,* Dent, 1987.

Rodney Castleden, *The Making of Stonehenge*, Routledge, 1993.

Christopher Chippindale, *Stonehenge Complete (Revised Edition),* Thames and Hudson, 1994.

R. Cleal, K. Walker & R. Montague, *Stonehenge in its Landscape: Twentieth Century Excavations*, English Heritage, 1995.

Rodney Legg, *Stonehenge Antiquaries*, Dorset Publishing Company, 1986.

David Souden, *Stonehenge: Mysteries of the Stones and Landscape*, English Heritage, 1997.

Avebury:

Aubrey Burl, *Prehistoric Avebury (Second Edition)*, Yale University Press, 2002.

Paul Devereux, *Symbolic Landscapes: The Dreamtime Earth and Avebury's Open Secrets*, Gothic Image, 1992.

Lynda J. Murray, *A Zest for Life: The Story of Alexander Keiller*, Morven Books, 1999.

Joshua Pollard & Andrew Reynolds, *Avebury: The Biography of a Landscape*, Tempus, 2002.

Rick Peterson, 'Thomas Twining's Roman Avebury', *The Wiltshire Archaeological and Natural History Magazine 96*, 210–213, 2003.

Isobel Smith, *Windmill Hill & Avebury: Excavations by Alexander Keiller, 1925–39*, Clarendon Press, 1965.

Peter Ucko, Michael Hunter, Alan J. Clark & Andrew David, *Avebury Reconsidered From the 1660s to the 1990s*, Unwin Hyman,1991.

General:

Lesley and Roy Adkins, *The Handbook of British Archaeology*, Constable, 1998.

John Aubrey, *Monumenta Britannica*, vols 1 and 2, eds. J. Fowles and R. Legg, Dorset Publishing Company, 1980, 1982.

Janet and Colin Bord, *Mysterious Britain: Ancient Secrets of Britain and Ireland*, Thorsons, 1995.

Mark Bowden, *Unravelling the Landscape: An Inquisitive Approach to Archaeology*, Tempus, 1999.

Aubrey Burl, *Rites of the Gods*, J. M. Dent & Sons, 1981.

Aubrey Burl, *From Carnac to Callanish: The Prehistoric Stone Rows and Avenues of Britain, Ireland and Brittany*, Yale University Press, 1993.

Aubrey Burl, *A Guide to the Stone Circles of Britain, Ireland and Brittany*, Yale University Press, 1995.

Aubrey Burl, *Great Stone Circles: Fables, Fictions, Facts*, Yale University Press, 1999.

Aubrey Burl, *The Stone Circles of Britain, Ireland and Brittany*, Yale University Press, 2000.

Julian Cope, *The Modern Antiquarian: A Pre-Millennial Odyssey Through Megalithic Britain*, Thorsons, 1998.

Michael Dames, *The Silbury Treasure: The Great Goddess Rediscovered*, Thames and Hudson, 1976.

Glyn Daniel, *Megaliths in History*, Thames and Hudson, 1972.

Paul Devereux, *Places of Power*, Blandford, 1990.

Paul Devereux, *The Illustrated Encyclopedia of Ancient Earth Mysteries*, Cassell, 2000.

Paul Devereux, *The Sacred Place: The Ancient Origin of Holy and Mystical Sites*, Cassell, 2000.

James Dyer, *Discovering Prehistoric England: A Gazetteer of Prehistoric Sites*, Shire Publications, 2001.

Miranda J. Green, *Exploring the World of the Druids*, Thames and Hudson, 1997.

Richard Hayman, *Riddles in Stone: Myths, Archaeology and the Ancient Britons*, The Hambledon Press, 1997.

David E. Johnston, *Discovering Roman Britain*, Shire Publications, 2002.

Rodney Legg, *Stanton Drew: Great Western Temple*, Wincanton Press, 1998.

John Michell, *Sacred England: A Guide to the Legends, Lore and Landscape of England's Sacred Places*, Gothic Image, 1996.

Paul Newman, *Lost Gods of Albion: The Chalk Hill-Figures of Britain*, Sutton Publishing, 1997.

Alastair Oswald, Carolyn Dyer and Martyn Barber, *The Creation of Monuments: Neolithic Causewayed Enclosures in the British Isles*, English Heritage, 2001.

Gerald Ponting, *Callanish & Other Megalithic Sites of the Outer Hebrides*, Wooden Books, 2002.

Jacqueline Simpson and Steve Roud, *A Dictionary of English Folklore*, Oxford University Press, 2000.

Geoffrey Wainwright, *The Henge Monuments*, Thames and Hudson, 1989.

Peter Woodcock, *This Enchanted Isle: The Neo-Romantic Vision from William Blake to the New Visionaries*, Gothic Image, 2000.

Ann Woodward, *British Barrows: A Matter of Life and Death*, Tempus, 2000.

Index of Sites and Places
in the Engravings

Ackling Dyke (Dorset) 17

Avebury (Wiltshire) 45–77
    Beckhampton Avenue 67, 68
    Cove, The 53, 58, 59
    Earthwork 63
    Entrance 56
    'Groundplot' 45
    Northern Circle 53
    Obelisk 60&61,
    Sanctuary, The 54& 55, 71
    Southern Circle 62
    West Kennet Avenue 63, 67

Bath (Somerset) 98

Boscawen-Un (Cornwall) 117

Bryn Gwyn Stones (Anglesey) 121

Burrough-on-the-Hill (Leicestershire) 106

Bush Barrow (Wiltshire) 37

Callanish (Isle of Lewis, Outer Hebrides) 116

Countless Stones, The (Kent) 107, 108–9, 111

Cranborne Chase (Dorset) 17

Devil's Arrows, The (North Yorkshire) 122–3

Devil's Den, The (Wiltshire) 76, 77

Figsbury Rings (Wiltshire) 89

Fosse Way, The (Nottinghamshire) 103

Glastonbury (Somerset) 90&91

Holbeach (Lincolnshire) 87, 104

Kit's Coty House (Kent) 107, 110

Lake Barrow Cemetery (Wiltshire) 35

London 97

Lough Gur (Co Limerick, Ireland) 120

Lyme Regis (Dorset) 102

Marlborough (Wiltshire) 84

Marlborough Mound, The (Wiltshire) 83, 84

Maumbury Rings (Dorset) 94, 95

Meini-Gwyr (Carmarthenshire) 117

Merry Maidens, The (Cornwall) 117

Mill Barrow (Wiltshire) 73

Morgan's Hill (Wiltshire) 49, 52

Newgrange (Co Meath, Ireland) 120

Nine Stones, Winterbourne (Dorset) 118

Oldbury Castle (Wiltshire) 15, 52, 92

Old Sarum (Wiltshire) 38, 89, 99, 100–1

Raw Dykes (Leicestershire) 86

Rollright Stones (Oxfordshire) 46, 47, 48,

Salisbury (Wiltshire) 38, 89, 101

Shelving Stones (Wiltshire) 75

Silbury Hill (Wiltshire) 54–5, 66, 69, 70,

St Albans (Hertfordshire) 88

South Cadbury Castle (Somerset) 93

Stanton Drew (Somerset) 113, 115
       Cove 114

Stonehenge (Wiltshire) 13–39
    'Area' 31
    Altar Stone 20, 29, 30
    Avenue 31, 32, 33
    'Cell' 20, 24, 25, 28
    Cursus 34
    'Goundplot' 22

Thorpe by Newark (Nottinghamshire) 103

Trundle, The (West Sussex) 93

Vespasian's Camp (Wiltshire) 16

Waden Hill (Wiltshire) 66

Waltham Cross (Essex) 85

Wansdyke, The (Wiltshire) 15

West Kennet Long Barrow (Wiltshire) 74

Wilton (Wiltshire) 83

Windmill Hill (Wiltshire) 63

Woodyates (Dorset) 17

Neil Mortimer was born in Bristol and brought up in Plymouth, Devon. He is the former editor of *3rd Stone* magazine and a founding editor of the journal *Time and Mind*. He has been a columnist for the magazines *Fortean Times* and *British Archaeology*, and is the main member of the elemental psychedelic band Urthona (www.urthona.co.uk). He lives with his family on the edge of Salisbury Plain.

Lightning Source UK Ltd.
Milton Keynes UK
UKHW03f1819251018
331213UK00006B/227/P